Difficult Moments in Child Psychotherapy

With contributions by

Paul L. Adams, M.D.
University of Texas Medical Branch
Galveston, Texas

Jules Bemporad, M.D.
Harvard Medical School
Boston, Massachusetts

Irving N. Berlin, M.D.
University of New Mexico School of Medicine
Albuquerque, New Mexico

Norbert B. Enzer, M.D.
Michigan State University
East Lansing, Michigan

Clarice J. Kestenbaum, M.D.
Columbia College of Physicians and Surgeons
New York, New York

Melvin Lewis, M.D.
Yale University
New Haven, Connecticut

John F. McDermott, M.D.
University of Hawaii
Manoa, Honolulu, Hawaii

Kenneth S. Robson, M.D.
Institute of Living
Hartford, Connecticut

John E. Schowalter, M.D.
Yale University
New Haven, Connecticut

James E. Simmons, M.D.
Indiana University Medical Center
Indianapolis, Indiana

Edward Sperling, M.D.
Albert Einstein College of Medicine
The Bronx, New York

Difficult Moments in Child Psychotherapy

Stewart Gabel, M.D.
Cornell University Medical College
New York Hospital—Westchester Division
White Plains, New York

Gerald Oster, Ph.D.
University of Maryland
at Baltimore

and

Cynthia R. Pfeffer, M.D.
Cornell University Medical College and Child Psychiatry Inpatient Unit
New York Hospital—Westchester Division
White Plains, New York

Illustrations by

Rita Marlier

JASON ARONSON INC.
Northvale, New Jersey
London

Library of Congress Cataloging-in-Publication Data

Gabel, Stewart, 1943–
    Difficult moments in child psychotherapy / by Stewart Gabel,
Gerald Oster, and Cynthia R. Pfeffer ; illustrations by Rita
Marlier.
        p. cm.
    Originally published: New York : Plenum Medical Book Co., c1988.
    Includes bibliographical references and index.
    ISBN 1-56821-043-4 (pbk.)
    1. Child psychotherapy.   2. Psychotherapist and patient.
I. Oster, Gerald.   II. Pfeffer, Cynthia R.   III. Title.
    [DNLM: 1. Psychotherapy—infancy & childhood.   2. Physician—Patient
Relations.   WS 350.2 G112d 1988a]
RJ504.G27   1993
618.92'8914—dc20
DNLM/DLC
for Library of Congress   93-10596

Manufactured in the United States of America. Jason Aronson Inc. offers books and cassettes. For information and catalog write to Jason Aronson Inc., 230 Livingston Street, Northvale, New Jersey 07647.

Foreword

> The evil that men do lives after them.
> The good is oft interred with their bones.
>
> (Shakespeare)

It is said in our case reports that it is the opposite:

> The evil that men do is buried in the record room.
> The good is oft reported at national meetings.
>
> (Philips)

All of us recall case reports in which the therapist makes a telling interpretation, the constipated youngster returns home, and at the next visit, all is changed. We all yearned for those moments and how seldom they occurred. This volume provides a service to all those who await the magic moment. Psychotherapy with children is difficult, and the resolution of problems achieved slowly. There are difficult moments—moments that need resolution for therapist or child.

This volume provides personal experiences of the most experienced child and adolescent psychiatrists who illustrate common experiences that awaken memories. How often the child does the unexpected, whether in the waiting room or in the playroom. The teacher wishes to demonstrate something to the patient, and the patient remains silent and immobile or races away and the teacher is dismayed. Luckily, it is not only the difficult that enchants but also the tender.

We owe much to those teachers and patients who taught us well. Some personal experiences come to mind. The retarded child whose parents insisted on institutionalization, who stole from the playroom a small car. When I saw him 2 years later on a crowded ward, he lifted the pillow of his bed and there was the small car. An impulsive destructive youngster who, ready to throw a block, stops and utters, "You want me to say what I feel and not throw it." A little girl who telephoned and, when the therapist's wife answered, said, "I hate you. Drop dead." The abused child who whispered to me at a court hearing, "Don't let them send me home." Or the 3-year-old who wanted to show me her "pee pee" because her father "puts his 'wee wee' in my 'pee pee.'" When I asked how she knew that, she informed me that her mother tells her every day. The incidents are legion. They confound and propound; they amuse and confuse. But above all, they teach, and we learn. We learn by listening and watching as our patients play or speak. In their silent courage, they tell us of their suffering—a child of an alcoholic, a frightened phobic youngster, an anorexic depressed girl, an encoporetic, and all others who enter our portals. It is our life work and provides the best of emotional and intellectual rewards. The authors wisely note:

> . . . through the challenges and opportunities that difficult moments present, both personally and professionally, they offer the opportunity for growth as individuals and as professionals. (p. 135)

This volume provides a wealth of learning. It is for all to enjoy.

Irving Philips

Preface

We believe that doing psychotherapy with children can be both enjoyable and productive. We also believe that some of our colleagues who do psychotherapy with adults disagree with us, especially about child-centered psychotherapy being enjoyable. Although there are undoubtedly many reasons that clinicians choose to never again do therapy with children after their introductory experiences with younger patients in general psychotherapy training programs, our feeling is that some clinicians are prematurely driven from child-centered psychotherapy by actual or fantasized "disasters" that can or may occur in sessions with children. The child who folds his arms across his chest and defiantly says "No" when the therapist comes to the crowded waiting room and asks the child to come with her to the therapy room is one example. Another is the child who infuriates the therapist by taking the green Magic Marker and using it to write his name in big letters—first on the desk, then on his arm, and finally on the wall of the office.

These difficult moments in sessions with children are usually the focus of seminars or supervisory sessions only after the fact. Books, classes, and lectures are usually devoted to such topics as psychological theories, particular approaches, underlying meanings, or particular techniques to elicit unconscious material. This book does not take this approach. It is concerned with difficult moments that actually occur during child-centered psychotherapy sessions and with ways of dealing with them or preventing them from becoming disasters.

In writing this book, we have drawn on our own and various colleagues' personal experiences in doing, supervising, and being supervised in psychotherapy with children. We present a number of clinical vignettes—both hypothetical (in Chapter 1) and actual (in Chapter 3)—based on our experiences and those of others in order to provide strategies for understanding and dealing with difficult moments that inevitably arise in psychotherapy with children. The vignettes are written in a manner that is sometimes lighthearted and always intended to, in effect, confront the reader with the difficult moment, so that he or she must try to arrive at appropriate solutions as the "story" unfolds. It is our hope that these experiences will be helpful to the child psychotherapist.

We do not favor one conceptual approach or therapeutic stance to the exclusion of others. We do believe, however, that difficult moments can be handled best by understanding several points. First, it is helpful to think of action and behavior as symbolic. That is, a patient's behavior is an overt manifestation or representation of an internal feeling, need, reaction, or conflict.

Second, behavior is purposeful and has meaning, often in the context of interpersonal relationships. The child who will not leave your office at the end of the session, despite your reminders, urgings, and fantasies of pulling the child's arm from its socket, is conveying something to you about his or her perception of the relationship and need to be in some way involved with you.

Third, embarrassment, confusion, anger, or frustration in difficult situations with children in therapy is nearly universal and must be personally acknowledged. To have a youngster pounding on your office door while you are speaking confidentially to the child's parents in the waning moments of the hour is frustrating at best. The child's symbolic and purposeful communication obviously needs to be considered in dealing with and understanding the situation. Your anger and embarrassment at not being able to think of the "right" thing to do at the time—as you perceive yourself looking foolish and incompetent to the child's parents—are understandable, if not extreme, and should not be experienced with too much self-criticism. The ability to not take oneself too seriously during difficult moments (or when thinking about them beforehand or afterward) goes a long way in making work with children more enjoyable.

Fourth, there are often no "right" answers about how difficult moments might have been avoided or managed. An angry, depressed, 12-year-old boy recently came to an evaluation with great reluctance. He refused to say anything other than his name and that he was not going to talk to anyone. The therapist assured herself from the parent's history that the boy was not a physical danger to himself or to others. Then, after waiting for 10 minutes, she told the boy and his parents that he was not ready for therapy and that he should return when he realized he had problems and needed help with them. A colleague of this therapist was aghast on being told about the incident. His view was that the youngster should have been told that it was alright not to talk if he did not want to, but that sessions would nevertheless be scheduled for him twice a week. He would be required to come to the sessions, and he could talk or play or be silent with the therapist as he wished. Here we see two totally different approaches from two respected clinicians. There are insufficient data on outcome in child-centered psychotherapy to say dogmatically that one therapist was right and one was wrong. We believe, as do all committed therapists, that therapy is helpful for many children, but it is uncertain exactly what the helpful ingredients are.

Fifth, in difficult moments, common sense, concern for the child, and practical approaches are to be emphasized. One-sided theoretical stances and absolute positions are sometimes taught in seminars, books, and lectures by various seers and gray eminences in the field. We believe that for our readers, and for ourselves, common sense and practical approaches are invaluable.

Sixth, contrary to what is often felt at the time, difficult moments are frequently not catastrophes. Such moments may be horrendous or disastrous only in the mind of the therapist; they may be beneficial or produce entirely different reactions in the child and in his or her parents. For example, Dr. Angry Redface, a friend and colleague, felt he would never have any clout with Billy or Billy's mother after the 6-year-old had run to the water fountain, gotten a mouthful of water, and "playfully" smiled and spit some of the water onto the doctor's shirt as the doctor was talking to Billy's mother. It was only during the next therapy session that Dr. Redface realized in talking with Billy's mother about the incident that she had been acutely embarrassed by what Billy had done. She felt that Billy's actions reflected negatively on her as a mother. She was not critical of the doctor's inability to anticipate or avoid this uncontrolled outburst. If anything, it seemed that Billy's mother had actually developed a stronger alliance with Dr. Redface because he had not hit Billy or refused to see him after the incident. She felt that Dr. Redface and she had both now experienced Billy in similar ways, and she felt comfort in sharing her burdens. There are relatively few moments or situations in child psychotherapy that are true disasters in the sense of being irremediable or setting the therapy on an irreversible downhill course.

Seventh, but perhaps foremost, difficult moments are more easily endured and made more productive by the ability to have empathy for the child and his or her feelings, reactions, and predicament. Considering the child's behavior and reactions from the child's point of view and being able to convey concern and sensitivity to that point of view will go a long way therapeutically regardless of the difficult moment. This approach will also help put the focus of the problematic moment where it should be: on the needs the child is expressing voluntarily or involuntarily by making the therapist feel inadequate and helpless.

Enough said in the way of an introduction. This is really a book of concrete and specific strategies that is intended to calm the pounding hearts of therapists anticipating difficult moments in work with child patients.

This book was purposely kept short and concise enough to be read at a few sittings. These spare hours may become available at various times: during the week before you see your first child psychotherapy case, between sessions of a particularly difficult therapeutic course with one patient, or when you return home and experience pangs of frustration and anxiety about what you have or have not done to maintain therapeutic progress after encountering a difficult moment.

Stewart Gabel
Gerald D. Oster
Cynthia R. Pfeffer

White Plains, New York
and Rockville, Maryland

Contents

Difficult Moments
in Child
Psychotherapy

1

Difficult Moments

This chapter presents 24 clinical vignettes that are intended to illustrate numerous difficult moments that may arise in psychotherapy with children. They have been adapted from our experiences and the experiences of colleagues. We also present a number of possible ways of managing the difficult moments exemplified in the vignettes. Our approach in this chapter is intended to be practical and straightforward. The vignettes are grouped in subsections that reflect broadly similar areas. This grouping is explained further in Chapter 2, in which we also discuss a more conceptual approach that may provide additional help in understanding difficult moments in psychotherapy with children.

DIFFICULT MOMENTS INVOLVING THE BEGINNINGS AND BENEFITS OF PSYCHOTHERAPY

When a Child Will Not Come to Your Office: The Anxious Child

The initial encounter between a child, and/or the parent(s), and therapist is always potentially difficult. Child, parent(s), and therapist inevitably experience anxiety when facing what is a new experience for all of them. There are several models for structuring the first meeting, including seeing the child before the parent(s), seeing the parent(s) before the child, and seeing parent(s) and child together in a family session. Difficult moments may may occur with each of these models. The following vignette illustrates a difficult moment that may occur when the child meets the therapist for the first time.

Stanley is a 6-year-old boy who has been referred for evaluation to the mental-health clinic by his mother at the urging of his first-grade teacher. Behavior problems have included defiance, angry outbursts, inattentiveness, and fighting in school. Stanley's mother spoke to the intake worker in charge of referrals, and it was agreed that you would evaluate Stanley and another member of the evaluation team would see his mother.

You have reviewed the written material, which, as often is the case, is quite skimpy. It is 2 P.M., and the receptionist calls your office to say that Stanley and his mother are here.

You go into the waiting room and introduce yourself: "Hello, Mrs. Jones. Hello, Stanley. I'm Dr. Eager Learner. Mrs. Jones, I understand you've made an appointment to talk about some problems at home. Dr. Experienced will be talking with you later, Mrs. Jones. I'd like to get to know Stanley better now and talk with him."

You nod to Stanley, smile warmly, extend your hand to the door leading to the hallway and your office, and say, "Let's go and talk, Stanley."

But Stanley does not move. He sits frozen in his chair, looking terrified. You repeat your little talk, try to smile even more pleasantly, and encourage him to come. Now, however, he seems even more adamant; his face reddens, and he shakes his head "No" and tightens his grip on the arms of his chair.

Stanley's mother tries to help. She says, "Go on, Stanley," and presses her hand against his back. Stanley does not move. He has a peculiar expression on his face—part negative, part defiant, and part terrified.

What should you do? Running away is not acceptable. Crying is overreacting. Pulling Stanley by the arm is not advisable and not therapeutic. Leaving and calling for help is an honest statement of how you feel, but sells your own capabilities short. Remember, beginning therapy with a child is never easy and often involves surprises.

Try some of these strategies:

1. Lean a little closer to Stanley in a friendly, non-threatening way. Bend your knees so that you meet him eye-to-eye. You will be less frightening that way and not as much a large, looming monster.

2. Explain in slightly more detail what you will be doing. Emphasize that you will be talking and playing games and that you have a number of games to play with that Stanley can choose if he wishes.

3. Clarify details about the visit. Perhaps his mother has not explained what the evaluation is really all about despite the intake worker's phone preparation. Talk to Stanley directly and say that you and he will be together for a short while and then he will rejoin his mother, who will be talking to Dr. Experienced down the hall while you and he are talking. Emphasize that this is not the usual doctor's office, that (if true) no shots or blood tests are given here, and that (if true) there will be no physical examination. Say that you are a different kind of doctor, although to yourself you may now be thinking of checking out radiology residencies again.

4. If all these strategies do not work, accept it as a matter of course without conveying anger or frustration to parent or child. Say that since it is hard for Stanley to come to the office with you now, you would like to begin by seeing him and his mother together at first. Indicate to Stanley's mother that both Stanley and she should come to your office now. Dr. Experienced can join the three of you there when she arrives.

These strategies usually work. Supported by the presence of the parent, a child often willingly comes to the evaluator's office. There, a brief discussion and clarification of the presenting problem are often all it takes to make the child feel comfortable enough to stay alone with the clinician while the parent or parents are interviewed separately—if that is the procedure that has been decided upon. Preparation of the parent and child prior to the visit can also be very helpful.

In our hypothetical example, let us assume that Stanley still will not come. Your kindness, your patience, your support, your clarification, and your allowing his mother to join you have been to no avail. Stanley remains frozen in his chair.

5. Tell Stanley it is alright for him to remain in the waiting room for now if he wants, but that you would still like to talk to his mother and he can join you and her if he wishes when he feels like it. Tell him where your office is, offer to show him, and assure him that the receptionist can lead him to it if he forgets. Then usher his mother out with you and go to your office. Often, children like Stanley will either accompany you when they realize their parents are really leaving their presence or will follow only minutes behind. Stanley almost certainly does not want to be separated from his mother, even if it means having to be with you, and even if it means losing a measure of control by giving in to your unreasonable and unacceptable demands.

6. Okay, let us assume that Stanley is an exception. Mrs. Jones and you are now in your office, and you are reassuring her that Stanley is frightened but that he may be along soon, and in any case, the time can be used to learn more about the referral problems. But five minutes pass, then ten, and the only footsteps to approach your door are those of Dr. Experienced. You explain the situation as you three adults, two doctors and one mother, talk about the 6-year-old boy who is not there.

After a brief time, suggest to Dr. Experienced and to Mrs. Jones that you would like to return to the waiting area and talk to Stanley. You reason to yourself that Dr. Experienced can probably handle the parent evaluation alone!

Returning to the waiting area, you find Stanley still frozen in his chair, looking around anxiously. Explain to Stanley that Dr. Experienced has come and is talking to his mother. You are eager to get to know him and wonder if he would like to play some games with you in the waiting area. If he does not move, select one of the games in the room and ask Stanley if he would like to play it with you over by the table. If he indicates no, take it or some toy or other game over to where he is and begin playing by yourself, periodically encouraging him to join in.

You may have to continue this for some time. Ultimately, though, the chances are that he will come to feel enough at ease with you that you can successfully urge him into your office for more enticing games that you assure him are there, and not in the waiting area. It will likely take only a short time to build a relationship with Stanley sufficiently trustful that he will come with you, for it is a rare child indeed who will not come to your office for the evaluation after you have used these strategies for one or two sessions. Sometimes it takes a little longer, but you will be learning about Stanley as you interact with him, interview him, and play with him in the waiting room.

Occasionally, however, you will encounter a child who is extremely oppositional and will accede to almost none of your requests even when he or she is not as obviously anxious as Stanley was in this first encounter with a mental-health clinician. Children of this type, whose resistance does not stem from obvious overwhelming anxiety, may require additional strategies. They are often trying indeed, and they merit a few pages of their own.

When a Child Will Not Come to Your Office: The Oppositional Child

Okay, you have done really well with Stanley, the boy in the previous example. He now comes to see you on a regular basis, and a therapeutic alliance has been established. Your reputation in the clinic is becoming established, and the secretaries and clerks are openly talking about how your adept handling of the situation with Stanley avoided a yelling, screaming disaster or a stony-faced standoff.

They must have put a bug in the clinic administrator's ear, because Stanley's cousin, Stubborn Smith, is scheduled for an evaluation later this week, and you have been assigned the case. Stubborn's referral information sounds like Stanley's, and your confidence is building rapidly.

Stubborn comes with his parents, Mr. and Mrs. Smith. He is silent, negative, and determined. He doesn't appear quite as frightened as Stanley was, although first impressions, you reason, can be deceiving. Like Stanley, Stubborn also refuses to come into your office for the initial session. You go through the same procedure you followed with Stanley: reassurance, support, explanation, clarification, offering to allow the parents to come with him to the office to get started, joining him in play or activities or games in the waiting area to build rapport and decrease anxiety.

This time, however, the response is different. Stubborn fools you. By the end of the first session, his parents have returned from their meeting with the parent evaluator, and you are still in the waiting room trying to engage the boy in play, while he, unlike Stanley, has run around the waiting area, getting as far away from you as possible. Finally, Stubborn does sit down in the opposite corner, and begins playing with some Play Doh, a defiant look on his face—a look that is replaced by one of smugness and accompanied by a gleeful squeal whenever you approach and he runs to another corner of the room to play calmly with other children waiting for their appointments.

What to do? Try to make the best of a bad situation. Thank Mr. and Mrs. Smith for coming today and bringing Stubborn with them. Explain to them that you have learned a lot about Stubborn today by watching him play and seeing his actions, and you think that seeing him today will help you better understand his behavior at home and in school. Tell them, also addressing Stubborn, that you now have a sense of Stubborn's behavior and can see how there could be problems at home and at school if the situation is like you have seen it here today. Tell them that you have some ideas to help and that you think that Stubborn is acting the way he does because he has learned to deal with situations that make him nervous by saying "No" and refusing to do things. You and they are going to try and help him not be so frightened of situations and help him learn different ways to act. Advise the parents and Stubborn to come back next week. Say "Goodbye" to Stubborn as if it were not a joy to see him go.

Let us stop here and see what you predict: Do you think the parents will come back next week and bring Stubborn with them? Do you think they will not bring him because he has refused or because they are too embarrassed, but that they will come? Do you think that neither parents nor Stubborn will come? The authors, self-proclaimed optimists and admitted poor prognosticators, think one of the first two options will occur. The third option—that no one will return— is less likely if the parents have been properly supported in the first session, but can still be handled by a phone call to them.

In any case, the strategies to be employed are similar. If parents and Stubborn come together, you can try again to encourage him to come to your office with you. If he still will

not come, but you feel hopeful, you can again spend the session in the waiting room trying to engage him. With increasing time, however, you may risk encouraging his oppositionality. Sooner or later, you will have to try a new strategy.

Speak to the parents directly and alone in your office, perhaps with the parent evaluator present. Explain that you feel it important for Stubborn to learn that limits and controls on his behavior must be established, along with the need to understand the reactions and fears that make him so negative and resistant. Having decided your course of action beforehand, discuss with the parents one of the following options:

1. Tell the parents that you will need their help in getting Stubborn to comply with the evaluation and that in so doing, by working on this problem together, you will begin providing help for Stubborn and help for them in handling his behavior. Formulate, with the parents, a behavioral program with appropriate reinforcers and consequences for the "behavior" of Stubborn's coming or not coming to your office (or coming or not coming to the clinic if the second option has come to pass and they have not been able to get him to come to the clinic).

2. With the parents' permission, explain to Stubborn that if he does not come with you to your office, he will be carried in bodily (preferably by a parent, although you and other staff should be available to help). If he has refused to come to the clinic, he should be told that he will be taken there bodily for the appointment. If this is done, once in the office (making sure all breakable objects have been removed), put yourself between him and the door. Explain that you will not hurt him and he will not be allowed to hurt you, but that he will be spending the hour with you in the office and you would like to get to know him better and share some time with him. Show him your watch or a clock and tell him when his time

will be up. Do that each session, as the evaluation progresses into therapy. (Did you really think Stubborn would not need therapy after the evaluation?)

If the parents have not come for the appointment themselves, call them on the phone and discuss their reasons for not coming and their reactions to the first visit. Reassure them of your continued interest in working with Stubborn and with them. Emphasize that you agree help is needed and make it clear that you feel they were right to bring him to the evaluation, even though it did not work out as they had hoped the first day. Set up an appointment to talk to just them without Stubborn, and in that session explain the two strategies noted above.

The behavioral program that you work out with the parents in the first strategy should really include positive reinforcement for Stubborn's participating in the evaluation with you, an act that Stubborn does not find intrinsically reinforcing. Perhaps a promised trip to McDonald's, an ice cream cone, or a ball game after the visit would help. If no positive reinforcers are available, however (which may mean that he has been so successful at manipulating his parents, and they are so unable to set limits, that he seems to get whatever he wants anyway), try encouraging them to withhold the weekly McDonald's trip, the ice cream cone, or the promised ball game until after the visit. Behaviorial programs, when well thought out, are often remarkably effective.

Finally, if the parents are unable to find any reinforcers or appropriate consequences to induce Stubborn to make the desired visit, and refuse to get him to the clinic by physically carrying him, tell them to continue coming anyway. It is a good bet that a major part of the problem is their parenting style, which needs much work and understanding. As you work with them, perhaps with a behavioral program at first, you will learn more about them, the environment, and Stubborn. After a while, you will be able to reinstitute your request that he be brought to the clinic for further evaluation. It is likely that when the parents have been able to exert some control at home with your help, the next time you see Stubborn, he will be much more compliant.

When a Child Does Not Know What Happens in Therapy

Believe it or not, there are times when an evaluation moves smoothly, problems are clarified, and recommendations are made and accepted. If therapy is recommended, therapists sometimes find it difficult to know what to say to the child and how to set the agenda for the ensuing sessions.

Bobby, for example, is an 8-year-old boy who has been evaluated because of fighting at home and at school. You have done the evaluation and spoken with Bobby and his parents about the problem. You have recommended individual therapy for Bobby and child-focused guidance for the parents. You will be doing both aspects of the therapy. You plan to see Bobby once a week and his parents once a week.

How do you tell Bobby what therapy and therapy sessions are all about? You can begin by saying to him that during the talk you had with him and his parents last week, you told them your impressions of the problems they were having. You recommended that he have psychotherapy and that his parents be seen separately by you so that they may also have a special time to work on problems. Although you explained that he would be coming to see you once a week, you are not sure if he understood what you will be doing. You want to talk more about therapy now.

Ask Bobby what he thinks the two of you will be doing together each week and the purpose of the sessions. He probably will not say very much, but there is a chance he may tell you a great deal about his expectations, fears, hopes, and other feelings concerning the sessions. At times, a child's remarks in this situation may serve as a good starting point for talking with him or her about various issues and the family as well as a way of clarifying the more technical aspects of therapy.

Let us assume Bobby hasn't been too helpful and he answers your question about what he anticipates from your sessions either by saying "I dunno" or by remaining quiet fidgeting anxiously.

He has put the ball back in your court. Explain to him as simply and concisely as you can that you will be seeing him every week and have set aside this special time for the two of you to spend 50 minutes together. The purpose of the sessions is for you and him to work together so both of you can understand his feelings and problems. You tell him that he may talk about whatever is on his mind. If there is nothing he wants to talk about, that's okay. He may choose to play with any of the toys in the office. He may wish to do such things as draw pictures, play catch, tell stories, or play with puppets. You believe that by spending time together in this manner, the two of you can work to understand the problems he has had and to try to make things better for him.

Ask Bobby if he has any questions.

Ask him how he feels about what you have said. Chances are he will nod his head or say something like "Okay."

That is fine. You are ready to begin. Ask him what he would like to do now. Chances are he will get a toy or a game from the shelf or cupboard to play with. Soon, you will be playing together. After awhile, you may comment about his play, and then about his relationships with you and with his parents. The sky is the limit. Growth, change, perhaps insight, are on the way!

When a Child Will Not Talk

Jennifer is 7 years old. She has been referred to the psychiatry clinic for evaluation because of the onset of bed-wetting and social withdrawal following the separation of her parents six months previously.

Unlike your previous two evaluation cases, Stanley and Stubborn, Jennifer readily parts from her mother in the waiting area and comes with you to your office. You explain the purpose of the evaluation and plan to begin the session in a nonthreatening manner by asking her her age, address, school, and other information.

To your surprise, however, Jennifer will not talk! The referral information said nothing about any neurological problem, developmental delays, or elective mutism. You are confident she can talk and has talked previously. In fact, you remember passing through the waiting area a few minutes earlier and seeing Jennifer and her mother talking to one another. No, it is clear, she will not talk to you!

Well, try some reassurance. Although she does not look frightened, she almost certainly is. Explain again the purpose of the evaluation, clarify that her mother is now talking to someone else in the room down the hall, and tell her that she will be rejoining her mother in the waiting area in about 45 minutes.

Still no luck! She will not tell you her age, her teacher's name, why she is here, or anything else. You feel that being "reasonable" may help, and you emphasize that the evaluation is important to learn more so that you can suggest what might be needed to help her feel better at home. On the basis of the referral information (which you can partially share with her), you suggest that she may have been feeling unhappy recently. Go over the fact that the purpose of the evaluation and your talking to her is not for you or her parents to blame

her or punish her, but that you want to understand and try to help both her parents and her.

Still no go! All you have for your efforts is stony silence and a 7-year-old girl with downcast eyes who is fidgeting in her chair.

Remember that good verbal skills are a late acquisition developmentally and that they remain precarious in anxiety-producing or threatening situations. Give it another try, but do not panic. Tell Jennifer that almost all the children you see find it hard or scary to come to see a psychiatrist (psychologist, social worker, educational counselor, nurse) for the first time and do not always want to talk right away. Ask Jennifer what she thought coming to the clinic today was going to be like. Tell her that different children have different ideas about what it means to visit a psychiatrist in training, and often they are scared. You would like to know her reactions to it.

Perhaps these statements will be helpful in allowing Jennifer to talk. If not, there is still no need to be discouraged or to convey discouragement, frustration, or anger to her. Chances are she is feeling enough of all that for the both of you. Tell her it is alright with you if she does not talk right now. Explain that you have a lot of other things to do in your office that are fun and worthwhile and that you and she can spend time productively in various ways other than talking.

Point out the toys in the room; show her the crayons and paper, the puppets and dolls. Say that she is free to play with whatever she wants. Tell her that different children like different toys and remark, in a wondering or questioning tone, "I wonder what you'd like to play with?"

In most cases, that will do it. Jennifer may not talk right away, but she will likely soon be playing by herself with one object or another and then, either by her nonverbal invitation in the play, through occasional remarks of yours, or through parallel play on your part, the transition to shared play and then to verbal interchange will have been made.

What if it does not work that way, though, and Jennifer does not take you up on your offer to use the play material in your office? Wait a few minutes and tell her it is alright if she wishes to choose something to play with later when she feels more like it, but that you are going to begin to use some of the material now. Take some paper and crayons, Play Doh, or some very modest activity that you can do while still seated near Jennifer, and begin to work with it. Make something interesting or funny. Occasionally ask her her opinion or make a comment about what you are doing. Minimize the need for her to talk if she chooses to interact with you.

Chances are the ice will be broken in that way and you will begin interacting nonverbally and, later, verbally. If not, consider it a good sign that she has been able to remain in the room with you and continue as is for the full session. End the session by saying you were glad to have had a chance to spend time with her; you feel you have gotten to know her better and you will be seeing her again next week. By then, of course, you will have gotten more information about Jennifer from the evaluator who spoke to her mother, and you will have formulated additional hypotheses about her refusal to talk to you.

If Jennifer still refuses to talk to you next session, you can repeat the process discussed above, perhaps offering the same or additional reasons for her resistance. You might say, for example, "It seems like it must have been scary for you to think of visiting a resident in psychiatry. I wonder what you thought it would be like . . . it must have been really scary for you to come here last week and today. Some children are so scared that they make the mistake of thinking they aren't going to be allowed to go home. That's not true, of course, but some children act as if they believed it was."

Patience at this phase should ultimately prevail. After awhile, if your comments and statements do not make things less frightening for Jennifer, relax a bit yourself. You do not want to have to do all the work, and pressing interpretations or reassurance too much will not be effective. Share the time with her, make periodic comments or facilitating statements, and enjoy whatever it is you are doing. It is in situations like this that one of the authors rediscovered his long-unpracticed artistic talents.

While drawing a funny face as a means of engaging Jennifer, this trainee also had time to consider the model of evaluation advocated by his particular child psychiatry clinic. He wondered if a model that involved seeing family members together for an initial session might have allayed Jennifer's initial anxiety and reduced her resistance, thus allowing for earlier verbal participation and relationship-building. That model, as it turned out with subsequent cases, eased the evaluation process considerably.

When a Child Announces a Desire to Stop Treatment

Determining whether there have been benefits to a psychotherapeutic intervention is timely and important to a multitude of those concerned, including the child, the parents, the school, and copayers. Gathering a baseline of information on the child through parental and school reports in areas such as behavior, moods, interests, and sibling and peer interactions makes treatment planning easier and facilitates the development of goals and objectives for effective intervention. In developing these criteria, it is also helpful to include the child's own appraisal of school and home life. By having stated goals from the beginning of therapy, one can refer back to these goals when questions are raised concerning whether to continue treatment.

Goals can be conceptualized along several dimensions. One dimension focuses on concrete symptom and behavioral change, such as a 75% reduction in bed-wetting, no more than two temper outbursts per week, or no more than one "negative" report from teachers in two weeks. Another dimension focuses on understanding conflicts or reactions within an individual and how these conflicts or reactions result in mood states, specific behaviors, and interpersonal problems.

The following example combines aspects of both these approaches with a stronger emphasis on concrete symptom or behavioral change. It emphasizes the need to consider the importance of defining goals early in treatment as a means of assessing progress in therapy.

Mary, age 9, was initially brought for therapy by her mother because of chronic bed-wetting, refusal to go to school, and throwing food at her new baby brother. As part of the evaluation, you asked her parents to complete behavioral rating forms that included a variety of behaviors such as temper outbursts, not listening, nightmares, stealing, toileting, and relationship to siblings. You also sent a similar form to the school (with the parents' and child's permission) to obtain further information. The school form also had items related to school attendance, activity level, general distractibility, peer relationships, completing class assignments, and compliance to instruction. With this fund of data, your clinical evaluation, and perceptions from Mary on her problem areas, you set forth in treatment, confident that you had defined a number of workable goals that you and Mary would pursue. These goals included decreasing the number of attacks on her brother, reducing the times per week that nocturnal bed-wetting occurred, decreasing the number of absences from school, and improving grades and peer interactions.

During the first six months of therapy, you have been pleased to learn from her mother and teacher that there has been some observable improvement in Mary's behavior. Also, through your own sessions with Mary, you have sensed that she is becoming more aware of the feelings surrounding the birth of her brother and is better able to express these feelings in talking to you about them and in her play. Nonetheless, when Mary came for her regular appointment last week and announced quite abruptly, "I don't think I will have to come to therapy after this week," you were flabbergasted. Although treatment had been going well, you had thought that further improvement needed to take place before you could plan a "proper" termination in several months.

"Why," you wondered, "is Mary so anxious to leave therapy so quickly . . . especially when things are just beginning to go so well!"

You have wondered why Mary has now brought up her desire for termination and have considered the possible reasons that additional resistance is emerging at this point.

You tell Mary that you are glad she is willing to discuss her feelings about the therapy with you and that you would like to talk to her further about how this decision was made. You also relay to her that you know that she has been doing well and that the reports from her mother and teacher have been positive. However, you still want to find out how this decision was arrived at and whether Mary and her mother had discussed it together.

As you are thinking about the various possible reasons the termination issue has arisen now, such as whether you said something at the end of the last session that offended the mother, you fail to realize that Mary has brought with her the paper upon which all her stated goals and objectives are delineated. She now hands it to you. As you examine the sheet of paper, you discover that Mary has summarized her own, her mother's, and her teacher's accounts of her behavior over these months. You sense that even though in your own clinical judgment you would prefer to continue treating Mary in order to feel more confident about the stability of her behavioral improvement, she has accomplished the initially stated goals.

With this confirmation about the actual changes Mary has made, you begin to further explore with her how she views things at home and at school and how she feels about ending therapy. She appreciates the fact that you can also see her improvement in the behavioral summary that she has brought into the session. She also tells you that she and her mother had discussed ending therapy several times over the past couple of weeks and how proud her mother is of the changes that she had made in her behavior. Upon hearing this, you are more comfortable with Mary's desire to terminate. Although you still do not give a definite answer to Mary about continuation in treatment, you do invite her mother into the session so that the three of you can discuss the matter. In fact, during the discussion, everyone agrees to a trial without regular appointments, but with some telephone contact and a plan to meet again for a follow-up visit in three months.

Evaluating and assessing the progress made in therapy has always been a complicated task, one that is beset by methodological and subjective problems. Subjective reports by children, parents, and teachers, and even data that are more objective, like school grades, all have limitations. Statements from children or the significant adults in charge of their care are often biased because of emotional attachments or their own vested interests in wanting to see positive, negative, or no change. When more formalized measures such as behavior-rating forms are employed in assessing therapeutic change, they may not be sensitive enough to reflect improvement or failure.

When you are deciding whether to continue working with a child or when some outside agency wants a progress report, you should gather information from several sources. Your judgment should be as unbiased as possible. Questions to be asked include: What benefits to the child are you providing by continuing the relationship? Have the presenting problems subsided? What will happen to the child if you discontinue the relationship? In addition, some systematic way of assessing change should have been instituted. This can be in the form of periodic ratings completed by the parents, the teacher, and the child. Finally, changes are easier to see when goals are clearly articulated early in the therapy and a systematic assessment of the changes is obtained at a prearranged time.

DIFFICULT MOMENTS INVOLVING RELATIONSHIPS IN PSYCHOTHERAPY

When a Child Asks Personal Questions

Normally, children are inquisitive and curious. Asking question of parents is typical of young children. Some parents find these interactions taxing, while others feel excitement, pride, and stimulation. For the child psychotherapist, too, children's questions present a number of important issues, as the following example aptly illustrates.

Penny Personal is referred to you because of her reluctance to go to school and her worries that other children do not like her. She is an intelligent 6½-year-old child who appears very animated, cheerful, and strong-minded. Her mother feels frustrated by Penny's frequent demands for toys and her failure to follow directions. Penny's father is very proud of his daughter's brilliance, spirit, and appreciation of life. Both parents are alarmed by their daughter's socialization problems at school.

Penny's parents met you for an initial session and then spoke extensively with her about her own future visit with you. Penny wanted to know if you were nice and if her mother could be present in the room when Penny met you. At the first meeting, Penny seems enthusiastic but shy when you introduce yourself to her. She carries several dolls into your office and sits down in a chair as she cuddles a large doll in each arm. She is very pretty, but reserved and mildly anxious. You immediately find her to be appealing, and you look forward to working with her. Penny shows you her dolls and tells you their names. You note that she has a keen sense of interpersonal poise. She tells you that her parents told her that you were pleasant and that you had long brown hair and were pretty. You feel pleased that she is positive toward you, and you predict that her attitude will enable beneficial therapeutic work.

Immediately, Penny expresses strong curiosity about you. She asks numerous questions in rapid-fire succession: Are you married? Do you have children? Do you have a girl? Where do you live? These questions are expectable and appropriate in certain situations. In ordinary social circumstances, there is no doubt that you would respond openly and directly. But what is appropriate in a psychotherapeutic situation?

Some psychoanalytically oriented therapists argue that the patient's knowledge of the therapist's real circumstances is not essential and may actually inhibit analyzing the patient's fantasies and the meaning the patient ascribes to the therapist. However, in most types of psychotherapy, completely withholding personal information about oneself is never fully realized and may not be necessary. Usually, a therapist attempts to assess the context of the questions and decides whether a factual answer is indicated and whether further exploration of the meaning of the question is desirable. This decision must be made quickly and depends on the timing and context in which the question arises. Penny, for example, after answering a question about friends in her neighborhood, stops stroking her doll's long brown hair, looks up, and asks, "Has you hair always been brown?"

"What makes you ask that?," you respond.

"I don't know," Penny says. After a brief pause, she begins to talk about her friends in the neighborhood again. A moment later, however, she stops, looks up, and asks if you have any children.

"Why do you ask that?," you respond again.

"I don't know," she says, and looks down.

It seems to be time to show Penny that you care about her questions and take them seriously, but that you mean to set limits on what is appropriate in your sessions. You say, "Penny, you seem to have a lot of interest in the way I am and in my life. I am also interested in you and your thoughts about everything that is important to you. In our time together, we will talk mainly about you and what you are thinking and feeling. I will not answer many of your questions about me because I think that *your* ideas and feelings should be what we are most concerned with here. I think I can help you best if we try to keep to your ideas and feelings without having to have me answer all of your questions."

Therapists often feel that withholding answers about their personal lives will antagonize the child or be viewed as rejection by the child. Child psychotherapists often experience maternalistic or paternalistic feelings toward their child patients. They wish to be viewed as empathic, benevolent care-givers. Any interaction involving the therapist that may be perceived as having potentially rejecting or frustrating qualities is particularly difficult. Therapists often feel confused and conflicted about how best to respond to seemingly benign personal queries. The foregoing dialogue illustrates one approach.

Depending on the circumstances, however, you may decide that it is alright to discuss certain personal factors with the child. These may include general answers to questions about where you live and whether you are married or have children. You may decide to answer questions related to these issues, but to limit the detail in your answers. This compromise lets the child know that you understand and empathize with his or her curiosity about you and that you are a person with a real life. As in the dialogue above, you may tell the child that you will not answer all questions, but want to discuss them and their importance to the child. This approach helps the child understand that the real facts about you are less important than your understanding how the child feels and thinks.

Another approach when questions begin appearing early in the therapy is to tell the child that he or she will have many questions about you and that you want to hear these questions. However, you will not answer many of them because answering the questions sometimes makes it less possible to explore their meaning. This approach sets limits on your providing factual information about yourself. This format is often easier to act on when you work with older children or adolescents than when you work with young children. Older youngsters often can understand why a question will not be answered better than younger children can.

Some therapists also find that careful revelations about their backgrounds or interests at times during the therapy may help to facilitate the process. A withdrawn, shy, and uncommunicative youngster wearing a T-shirt from McDonald's may be helped to gain trust in you by learning, for example, that you also like McDonald's Big Macs and are able to compare McDonald's with Burger King and Wendy's. Telling the child your own preferences may allow informal conversation and an opening to more in-depth therapeutic contact.

Throughout the therapeutic process, the child will be tempted to ask questions about you. This curiosity is multifaceted in relation to the evolving therapy. Your work in handling such questions must be flexible. For example, as treatment progresses, the child will probably realize that factual responses from you are less forthcoming. He or she may come to realize that this withholding is not rejection. The child will likely come to understand that the relationship with you is different from the relationship with other people.

When a Child Brings Food to the Session

In today's society, children are extensively exposed to a variety of inducements to eat. They experience the wonders of crackling cereal, appreciate the varieties of french fried potatoes and variously prepared and garnished hamburgers, and sample mounds and mounds of rainbow displays of ice cream flavors. Yet many children have conflicts that involve food. Furthermore, for all children, eating takes on meanings involving their ongoing interactions with family and other emotionally important people.

A psychotherapist working with children invariably has to deal with a myriad of issues pertaining to food and eating. One direct way that this issue becomes manifest is when a child brings food to the therapy session and also invites the therapist to join him or her in partaking of the food. The following two brief vignettes point out different aspects of a child's involvement with food during a therapy session. Specifically, they illustrate the importance of these acts within the context of the larger sphere of the child's psychological functioning.

Amelia is a pretty 8-year-old who begins therapy with you in September after returning from her first summer experience at overnight camp. She found the experience very upsetting because she missed her family and she did not like the other children. Now she is upset about starting third grade at school. Amelia's parents bring her to you because they have never seen Amelia so anxious about going to school. They tell you that Amelia's father insisted that she go to overnight camp but her mother was reluctant and preferred that Amelia go to day camp and then join her parents on a trip at the end of the summer. Both parents are dismayed about Amelia's anxiety and they blame each other for her problems. Nevertheless, they care very much about their daughter and are highly motivated to work with you to help her. It appears that Amelia's mother is deeply involved with her and perhaps overprotective and unable to easily separate from her daughter. The father seems to be hard working and away from the home a great deal.

On the first visit with you, Amelia brings a large cup of soda and some cookies. Amelia is a very friendly child. She tells you that she came to see you directly from her piano lesson and that she brought food because she was hungry. Amelia drinks the soda and eats the cookies without any inhibition. She is very talkative and provides a lot of information about her family, her worries at camp, and her reluctance to go to school. She asks if you would like to share some of her cookies. Although the cookies look good and seem quite tempting you decline her offer but not without some misgivings. Your are concerned that Amelia's offer to share food may mean she has symbolically offered to share herself, her

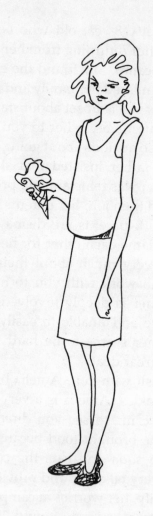

relationship with her mother, or at least a part of her presenting problem with you. Saying "No" may convey to her a
rejection of her needs. Accepting the cookie may allow her to
feel that you will share her problems with her. Yet, your
sharing food with Amelia is less desirable behavior than sharing feelings and thoughts which are the work of the
psychotherapy.

Finally, there are issues of personal likes and dislikes and
of control. If you do not like cookies or are dieting or do not
want to ruin your appetite before lunch, accepting cookies
may please Amelia but cause you to feel uncomfortable or
intruded upon. Often, there do not seem to be any right or
wrong answers. Some therapists might take a cookie or two
while establishing the relationship, but feel more comfortable
in declining the cookies after a relationship has been established later in the course of the psychotherapy when a more
complete discussion of food and its meaning can be had.

In Amelia's case, you decline her offer and tell her that
you are not hungry and that you appreciate her offer and she
can go ahead and enjoy the cookies. Since this is her first
meeting with you, it seems better to observe her behavior and
listen to her concerns. You do not think that any interpretation
about her eating is warranted at this time. Your goal is to
understand the meaning of the act of bringing food to therapy.

Amelia appears to be a relatively compliant child who is
competent and seems to trust you. She tells you that she is
worried about going to school this year because she does not
want to be teased by the other children. She worries that she
may be teased because this happened to her at camp. She
thought that the girls in her cabin were mean and they said
upsetting things to her. Amelia's parents told you that Amelia is generally shy with other children. Amelia tells you that
she feels more relaxed when her mother is with her. This
statement seems to corroborate your initial impression about

problems brought on by separation of Amelia from her mother.

You now hypothesize that Amelia's need for food in this first session is her way of symbolically having her mother with her at the session. She may be trying to decrease her anxiety and gain greater internal support for herself in the face of her mother's absence. It may also be that her offer to share her food is her wish to share with you the symbolic presence of her mother and the comfort it affords. You increasingly suspect that although Amelia is talkative and animated with you, she may also be anxious about meeting a strange person. Thus, you consider the possibility that the food brought into the session is a transitional phenomenon that creates a link between Amelia's wish to be protected by her mother and her competence in handling a new situation.

You wonder whether Amelia's father's insistence that Amelia go to summer camp was an effort to help her separate from her mother. Perhaps Amelia's worries about peers were evidence of her fears that "bad things" could happen if she were without her mother. Your formulation suggests in part that a child's act of bringing food to a session can have specific psychological implications. It may indicate something about the parent–child relationship. Rarely is it only a response to physiologically induced hunger. Rather than prohibit the bringing of food to the sessions when working therapeutically with children, it may be advantageous to allow this action and to determine how it may be related to important concerns that brought the child to treatment.

The second example is of a child who over a period of many weeks from the beginning of therapy never brought food to a session. It illustrates that her not doing so was as much a meaningful indication of her emotional state as was Amelia's doing so.

Cheryl was 11 years old when she began treatment. Her

parents sought help because Cheryl, an excellent student, was anorectic and prone to violent temper tantrums. When Cheryl was angry, she often hit her mother.

Treatment progressed slowly and appeared very arduous. Although she came regularly, Cheryl seldom talked. You remained calm and patient even though you felt frustrated at not being able to fully understand how she was feeling. Finally, you began to realize that Cheryl may actually have been appreciative of the opportunity to be with you and that perhaps what she was revealing through her taciturn manner was a need to be with someone who was empathic, but not intrusive. Perhaps her needs were for someone who could appreciate her even if she did not give encouraging indications of positive rapport.

As time went on, it became evident to you that Cheryl sensed your desire to be helpful to her. After several visits, she told you that she wanted to look at the games and toys in your toy closet. She found a chess set and invited you to play with her. This was the first evidence of a wish to interact with you more than minimally. Cheryl was an excellent chess player. She concentrated intensely and made moves carefully, as was also characteristic of her demeanor in treatment sessions. Her initial long periods of silence had been associated with her contemplative evaluation of you. She had been attempting to determine how you would respond to her. Finally, she made her first move at active involvement with you when she asked to use games.

Weeks passed and Cheryl continued to play chess with you. Intermingled with this play, there were brief conversations centered on her involvements in school. In meetings with her parents, you learned that her temper outbursts were diminishing. Cheryl expressed more interest in friends, began to baby-sit, and was planning to participate in a class play. You were pleased that Cheryl was less argumentative and more socially involved. During sessions, Cheryl gradually increased her repertoire of play activities. She used dolls and drawings and talked more extensively.

One day, she came to her session with a hamburger and soda. It was the first time she had brought food to a session or was willing to talk about food. She told you that she was hungry on her way to your meeting and that she used her allowance to buy the food. This act of bringing food to a session appeared to be a beginning of the process of exploring her eating disorder.

Your belief was confirmed over the next several sessions. Each time, Cheryl brought some type of food. In fact, one time she even offered you some. You accepted her offer and even complimented her on her choice of food. Discussion over the next several sessions showed that Cheryl's bringing food to the session with you was her way of indicating that she no longer had to control her impulses, feelings, and environment as strongly. She was able to show you that she was now developing a better sense of self and body image. This could all be shared with you through the act of eating in your presence.

These examples highlight the need for you to respond flexibly to a child patient while simultaneously evaluating the meanings of the child's behavior. With respect to bringing food to sessions, these two examples point out the various meanings that food and the act of eating have to children. A well-known nursery rhyme clearly suggests this, too, and can serve as a guiding theme in understanding the need to be flexible in dealing with children, whatever their concerns:

Peas porridge hot,
Peas porridge cold,
Peas porridge in the pot nine days old.

Some like it hot,
Some like it cold,
Some like it in the pot nine days old.

When a Child Wants to Bring Another Child to the Session

The child in therapy projects onto the therapist and the therapeutic situation a host of unconscious feelings, attitudes, and fantasies toward other people. Thus, the child's requests to bring someone into a therapy session can have many and very important meanings with respect to past and present interpersonal relationships. These requests also have important implications for shaping the course of therapy. The following example highlights the complexities of children's interpersonal relationships as they are focused on a request to bring a sibling to a session.

Brenda is 10 years old when she comes to you for help after making two suicide attempts with overdoses of aspirin. She repeatedly complains that she has no friends and that the other children tease her. Brenda is anxious when she is with other children. She either withdraws from playing with them or tries to boss them or control the games they play. She is pained by the trouble she is having with peers.

At home, Brenda often gets into fights with her 7-year-old brother. He is very verbal and assertive and has more social poise than Brenda. She feels helpless in not being able to match her brother's social acceptance. As a result, she often hits, pushes, and bullies him.

During therapy sessions, Brenda often speaks to you about her brother. She calls him a pest and speaks about wishing that he did not exist. During one session, however, Brenda surprises you by asking if she can bring her brother with her next time. You respond that you realize how important her relationship with her brother is and that you would

like to talk with her more about her request before deciding whether to include her brother in a session. You want to understand what she expects will happen if her brother visits. You specifically wonder and try to elicit from Brenda how this can be helpful to her: Does she want you to see how much of a nuisance he is? Does she want you to change him? Does she want you to help her respond to him?

Your questions stimulate discussion that immediately leads to conversations about peers. Brenda talks about being confused with friends and says that sometimes they remind her of her brother. She feels that they are "pushy" and that they tell her what to do. This makes her feel so angry that she does not want to be with them. She says that her angry feelings are almost the same as when she fights with her brother. This discussion elucidates the link between Brenda's feelings toward her brother and her problems with her friends.

Brenda's request to bring her brother to a session has been an organizing point for extensive discussions of her peer problems. For a time, she appears less interested in having her brother come to a session and is much more concerned with her relationships with peers. Your therapeutic plan at this point focuses on her own perceived needs. You develop a plan to promote interactions between you and Brenda that are similar to those between two friends. Thus, you play, compete, and express pleasure and/or anger as these responses seem appropriate within a context of peer interactions. Therefore if you play checkers, you plan to compete, to try to win, and to be able to disagree with her. This plan is in keeping with your concept of relating to her as a friend or peer. By doing this, you hope to help her develop better adaptive skills in peer relationships.

Periodically, in subsequent sessions, when peer relationships have improved, Brenda again mentions bringing her brother to a session. One day, her brother does arrive with her unexpectedly. This apparently occurred because Brenda's mother was unable to obtain a sitter for him. You make a number of observations in the waiting room. Brenda's brother is very alert, active, and verbal. He dominates interactions with Brenda. However, Brenda responds with a definite sense of big-sisterly empathy, patience, and direction. She does not show anger but does seem anxious, especially when her brother takes a "center-stage" role in their interactions.

When Brenda enters your office, she expresses excitement that you have met her brother. She tells you that he is very smart. Although she says he is always "bothering her," and she finds it difficult to have him around, she also seems proud and positive about him. You remind her that it is not easy to have an active little brother who sometimes demands things and is very bossy. You say that sometimes big sisters feel very angry and that they may wish that a younger brother did not exist.

Smiling, Brenda agrees with your statements and tells you about a number of troublesome encounters she has had with him. Brenda is quite relieved to be able to tell you about her wishes, which she feels are "bad" and "mean." She thinks that when she has these "bad thoughts," she also has trouble with friends. In this case, Brenda seemed satisfied for you to simply see her younger brother and all the trouble he could cause her.

Your delay in acquiescing to her wishes was most appropriate. It allowed you to analyze Brenda's fantasies, conflicts, symptoms, and adaptive skills. In fact, in most circumstances of individual psychotherapy with children, it is not essential to accede to the child's requests immediately. However, it is not contraindicated to meet other children whom the child wants to include in a session. It might have been helpful in this case to have a session or talk with Brenda and her brother so that interactions could be observed, clarified, and channeled more adaptively. An important point, however, is to have a clear idea of the framework and goals of the session and not to lose sight of who your patient is and what his or her needs are.

When a Child Asks You to Talk with the Parents

For the most part, psychotherapy is an intensive process that transpires between a patient and the therapist. In the case of children, the parents are involved to varying degrees. In most circumstances, the therapist sees the parents at periodic intervals in order to exchange information about the child's ongoing status and to counsel the parents about how they may understand and help promote the child's emotional needs. A complication may ensue, however, when a child asks the therapist to communicate specific information to the parents. Such a request has far-reaching implications, as the following example illustrates.

Scott, age 7, has been seeing you for several months. His teacher referred him to you because of his impulsivity and inability to pay attention. His schoolteachers felt exhausted by their extensive efforts to manage him in class. Often, it was necessary to remove him from the classroom and work with him individually in the library. His parents, especially his mother, are frustrated by the need to go to school to take him home when he is disobedient. Scott is currently in the second grade. Last year, although he exhibited similar behavior problems, his teacher was able to manage him. However, this year his behavior is worse, and his teacher cannot handle him in class every day. Furthermore, Scott's mother is very critical of him and attempts to impose strict limits on his behavior, with the result that she is overcontrolling with him. In response to her efforts, Scott becomes oppositional, angry, and defiant. This behavior precipitates an increase in his mother's tension, impatience, and hostility toward him. This vicious cycle is repeated and is aggravated by the necessity for Scott's mother to intercede on his behalf in problems with peers and schoolteachers.

Your diagnosis is that Scott has an attention-deficit/hyperactivity disorder. You institute treatment with psychostimulant medication. The medication greatly improves his concentration and some of his impulsivity. Yet his opposition and defiance are still disruptive. Although Scott's symptoms are much diminished, his mother sometimes continues to be excessively angry and verbally hostile. At times, her remarks to Scott are corrosively harsh. In contrast to his mother's responses, Scott is proud of his progress. He is compliant in taking his medication and is relieved that it is helping so much. For the first time, he is able to maintain adequate friendships.

One day, Scott comes to his session in a dejected state. At school the day before, he got into a fight with another boy, punching him in the mouth and cutting his lip. Scott was sent to the principal's office and told that if this happened again, he would be suspended. The principal tried to telephone Scott's mother, but she was not at home. Scott tells you that he is very frightened of his mother's reaction when she finds out what happened at school. He cries as he reveals this to you. He asks you to tell his mother about the fight at school.

Scott's marked distress is very compelling, and it is tempting to agree to meet with his mother. Nevertheless, you realize that there is much to be learned from this crisis, especially about the conflicts between Scott and his mother. You realize that you must decide whether or not to speak with Scott's mother at this session.

One plan is to spend the remainder of the session only with Scott and not to see his mother. This would make it possible to discuss the events at school more fully with Scott and to help Scott plan his approach to telling his mother about the day's events. The advantage of this plan is that it would make Scott totally responsible and autonomous in his actions and require him to accept the consequences of his behavior. The main disadvantage is that his mother's harsh reprimand and discipline may be characteristically unmodified or entirely uncontrolled.

Another plan is for you to take total responsibility for informing Scott's mother and for speaking with her about how she would like to respond to this information. An advantage of this plan is that you can devote a maximum amount of time to helping Scott's mother ventilate her reactions to this news and to understanding her perceptions about her son. A disadvantage of this approach is that Scott may develop strong feelings and fantasies about your omnipotence and ability to resolve problematic issues.

A third plan combines the two previous approaches and involves an immediate meeting with Scott and his mother. This will provide an opportunity to observe and respond to the mother–child interaction. Thus, the communication about the school day can commence in your office, a place in which all concerns can be outlined, analyzed, and managed in a more controlled way. It may help modify the conflicted interactions between parent and child that might otherwise ensue after the session. You can be a facilitator for more benign and beneficial interactions between the child and the mother. Another advantage is that you can assist Scott in making his difficult revelation to his mother.

You must decide quickly which plan to use. Two of the plans involve a deviation from the ongoing process of individual child psychotherapy. Nevertheless, you realize that psychotherapeutic work with children necessitates a flexible orientation. In this example, Scott asked for help directly from you: "Could you tell my mother about what happened to me at school yesterday?"

Scott's request is a distinct message that he is aware of the conflicts he has with his mother. An implication of his request is an acknowledgment of your ability to help him. At this moment, the therapy can focus on this aspect of Scott's problems, namely, his difficulties with his mother.

In many circumstances of child psychotherapy, a crisis situation may dictate that a special treatment format be used. In this example, had you delayed in responding to Scott's request, he may have perceived you as not caring or not responding to his needs. You therefore decided to meet with Scott and his mother, although your decision might have had additional implications for the treatment. For example, Scott's mother might react defensively or angrily to your now obvious favored status with her child, or Scott might come to view you as a direct ally in conflicts with his mother.

This example highlights the appropriateness of maintaining flexibility during the process of child psychotherapy. A child's request for you to tell a parent something must be evaluated within the context of a number of issues. Consideration must be given to what is currently happening in the therapy process, to what is occurring at present in the child's life, and to what the content and meaning of the request are to the child. A contrasting example to the previous one is one in which a child's request that you impart information to the parents indicates resistance to therapeutic progress. A 10-year-old boy's request that you talk to his parents about raising his allowance may be an attempt to manipulate the therapeutic process for inappropriate ends or a resistance to asserting age-appropriate independence. In such a situation, you may prefer to continue the discussion with the child about his request. In such a case, there would be little need to make an immediate decision to change the format of treatment. Instead, more time should be allotted in the session to consider the nature and meaning of the child's request.

When a Child Must Be Told about Abrupt Treatment Termination

The clinician treating children must realize that the termination of therapy is never easy and is often accompanied by a variety of responses by the child, the parents, and the therapist. Careful planning of the termination is critical. Abrupt or unexpected terminations complicate the process greatly, as the following example illustrates.

For the past year, you have been working on a weekly basis with Eric, an 8-year-old. Eric was initially referred for problematic behaviors stemming from his parents' separation several months prior to being seen for evaluation. His father had moved out of the area and had not visited him in three months. Presenting symptoms of temper tantrums and enuresis have subsided, and through the year's work you have established a close bond with Eric and have helped him identify feelings surrounding issues of separation. You have also provided him with alternative ways of expressing his anger and frustration.

However, you were not prepared for Eric's immediate and intense reaction when you told him that you were leaving the city in a few months, having just received an appointment at an out-of-town hospital. To your surprise, Eric immediately destroyed most of the creations he had worked on during the year and angrily left the room. Because you had waited until the end of the hour to tell Eric about the termination, it was not possible to get him back into the office.

At the time of his next appointment, Eric's mother called to cancel. She told you that Eric had been upset all week and that he had had several enuretic episodes.

Realizing that you had made a mistake in not telling Eric about the termination earlier in the session, and that the situation had been complicated by the need for premature termination of therapy, you call Eric to reassure him that you will still be his therapist until the final date. You also tell him that you feel bad about this upsetting news and that you wish to see him until the final day.

"Why should I," he yells, "when you are going away just like my father did?"

You tell him that you understand his feelings and that it is important for the two of you to meet to talk more about them. With this expression of your concern, Eric agrees to come to the next session.

During the next several sessions, you implement a strategy for terminating the therapeutic relationship with Eric. You again emphasize that stopping regular therapy sessions is extremely difficult for children and adults. You tell Eric that he has worked well in therapy and that stopping, especially so unexpectedly, is hard. You review with Eric the progress he has made, underlining his specific accomplishments. You discuss with him at some length the relationship he has had with you and how that has been important for him during the time he was feeling his father's loss so strongly. You use his reactions to the termination as a way of discussing in more depth his parents' separation and his father's unavailability. This process, although more abbreviated than desirable in Eric's case, allows therapy, support, and planning to continue to the end. It reassures Eric, his mother, and you that the work you and he have done together has been a beneficial and important experience. You tell him that you will think of him in the future and would like to know how he is doing.

At this time, many children will talk about visiting you or at least writing or calling you. Whether and how future contacts are made with a child may vary depending on the therapist's style and situation. In this case, you give Eric your forwarding address and say that although you will not be able to answer all letters, you would like to hear from him from time to time.

Finally, after acknowledging and working on these issues of separation during the next several sessions, the question of Eric's continuation in therapy arises. This is an important therapeutic issue. If you feel that treatment goals have been accomplished, it is well to discuss your feeling with the child and parents, and also to discuss with them their feelings about terminating therapy or continuing with another therapist. In the situation with Eric, the decision is made to stop therapy, at least for a time. You decide to highlight the end of the current therapy by having a ceremonial graduation. You award him a diploma, as you again emphasize his progress.

If, however, you feel that a child needs continued treatment, and the child and parents are agreeable, you would help arrange for a new therapist. Optimally, the child and parents would meet the new therapist before you leave, and you would help them in making the inevitably difficult transition.

When a Child Has Secrets with Dangerous Implications: The Suicidal Child

A secret is a child's personal treasure. The child owns it entirely until he or she wishes to share it with someone. Whether the secret is kept is determined by the meaning a child ascribes to the situational context and the relationships with the persons to whom the secret is relevant. Sharing a secret may enhance the bonds of a relationship. An example of this is when a child divulges a secret to someone and instructs the confidant not to tell anyone about it. When a child keeps a secret, he or she has control over others. For example, a child may state that he or she knows something but will not tell what it is. This statement is often fun for a child, and it arouses curiosity in those to whom it is made. The act of keeping a secret also involves a process of mastery for a child. In some circumstances, it involves a child's efforts to cope with difficult feelings, fantasies, behaviors, or experiences. Children classify secrets into "good" ones that have elements of surprise and fun and "bad" ones that relate to problem behaviors or fantasies.

The process of therapy with a child who has a secret is influenced by the content of the secret and especially by its implications. One type of secret that warrants strict and immediate attention is that which involves a child's wishes to hurt or to kill himself or herself. Such a secret may be classified as a "bad" secret. The following case illustrates this type of secret.

Sam is a 10-year-old who has severe learning problems. He feels insecure and worries about being teased by peers. He withdraws from group activities because he feels he is stupid. His friendships are limited because he feels most comfortable being with one friend at a time. He worries most when he has to go to parties or school social events. These situations make him feel unhappy and anxious. He openly tells you about these painful feelings. However, he does not tell you that he frequently thinks about killing himself. In fact, he has told no one about these fantasies. He has a plan that if he still feels this way by the time of his birthday next week, he will jump in front of the subway near his home.

You have been treating Sam for 2 months. As treatment has proceeded, Sam has begun to feel more trustful of you. He begins to indicate that he has an important secret, but is not willing to share it with you yet. You tell him that you are very interested in his ideas and feelings and that you hope he will soon feel comfortable enough to share all his ideas with you. You tell him that by sharing his most secret thoughts with you, he may begin to feel better and that you will be able to help him more. These statements help to relax Sam sufficiently for him to tell you about his suicidal fantasies.

Suicidal impulses are expressed by children of all ages, and any suicidal communication by a child should be considered very serious. Regardless of whether a child speaks about suicidal tendencies for the first time during the initial therapeutic meeting or after being in therapy for awhile, the approaches to management are similar. A child's statement about imminent suicide plans should alert the therapist to expand the dialogue so that the parents are included. Thus, the therapeutic management of a child's suicidal impulses may have to be carried out differently than plans for other types of interventions.

Management of a child's suicidal impulses must be rapid and decisive. A primary intervention is to assure the child's safety. In all circumstances, as noted above, the child's parents should be involved immediately. They need to be informed about the child's distressed state and to be integrated into the evaluation of the factors contributing to the child's suicidal tendencies and the planned therapeutic management of the urgent problem. In addition, extensive discussion with the child about his or her intentions, fantasies, and reactions to particular life circumstances must be pursued.

It is common for a child to tell the therapist about suicidal fantasies and to want him or her to keep this knowledge confidential. Sam is an example of this. He does not want you to tell anyone about his secret plan. His wish to maintain secrecy may involve his perception of you as a special person. A number of other fantasies may be related to his request for you to maintain secrecy. Sam may want to share something special with you, such as ideas about the meaning of life and death. He may wish you to know about the problems leading to his discomfort and wish you to explore whether other possibilities for change exist. He may perceive you as being omnipotent and able to rectify his problematic circumstances.

You realize that it is imperative that you respond immediately in a number of ways. You try to engage Sam in more extensive discussion about his suicidal fantasies. You ask a number of pertinent questions specifically about suicidal impulses. Among these questions are: Have you had the wish to hurt or kill yourself at any time before? Have you tried to harm yourself before? When did these ideas or acts occur? What was happening to you at home, in school, and with your friends at those times? What do you think will happen if you carry out these ideas now? Are you often sad, blue, anxious, or angry? Have you ever heard voices telling you to hurt yourself? Have you ever tried to get help when you had these feelings?

You tell Sam that harming himself is not the best way of solving his problems. You tell him that you can definitely help him with his painful and disturbing feelings. You tell him that you do not think that it is helpful to keep these ideas secret. You suggest, and if necessary insist, that it would be helpful if you and he speak with his Mom and Dad about his upsetting thoughts. This statement leads into the third aspect of intervention, which is to ask his parents to meet with you and him.

Fortunately, Sam's parents have brought him to the session and you can speak with them immediately. If Sam's parents had not been in the waiting room that day, you would have had to keep Sam with you and call them to come and meet with you to discuss Sam's suicidal mood. An alternative, if the parents cannot come to your office, would be to meet them at an emergency room or take Sam home, where the situation can be discussed further. Sam's parents must be informed that Sam has told you something very important.

In talking with Sam about informing his parents, you have decided that a family meeting would be appropriate. In your discussion of the upcoming session with Sam, he has asked you to inform his parents of the problem. Although it is usually best for a child to take some responsibility in talking to his parents about important matters, the urgency of this situation requires some flexibility in order to gain Sam's involvement in the session.

In the family session, you tell Sam's parents that it is important for them to know what Sam has told you today, namely, that he has been thinking of ending his life. You tell them that Sam's feelings about this must be taken seriously. You tell them that Sam has been feeling very sad and that you wanted them to know this so that they can help him to be safe and to feel better. You talk with them regarding their ideas about what may be contributing to Sam's distress. An important issue to be addressed in the session is how to plan approaches to maintain safety for Sam at this time. Sam and his parents must both be involved in this discussion of his safety, and all must feel that he is not imminently suicidal, or immediate hospitalization would be required. If you, Sam, and his parents agree that he is not acutely suicidal, outpatient measures may be in order. You suggest that Sam and his parents meet with you the next day. You tell them to call you if they have any other concerns before the next meeting. The main goal of this initial informing session is to work together to ensure Sam's safety and to begin a process of exploring what has led to his suicidal fantasies. This approach of working with Sam and his parents must be utilized throughout the period when his suicidal impulses are present. When these impulses resolve, therapy may be continued with less of a sense of urgency.

In some cases, however, a family may be resistant to working with you. The parents may not be able to appreciate the seriousness of the problem. The family may be stressed by many problems and therefore unable to provide a protective setting. In this situation, it may be necessary to hospitalize the child psychiatrically to provide a safe, protective, and structured environment in which evaluation of the child's problems can be undertaken.

Finally, work with a suicidal child always creates in the therapist intense reactions that may require consultation with a respected colleague about management of the child's therapy and/or individual exploration of one's own reactions by involvement in one's own psychotherapy. Conscious and/or unconscious fantasies about death, violence, loss, suicide, and sadness can affect a therapist's judgment.

It should also be emphasized that a crucial aspect of therapeutic work with a suicidal child is to foster continuous communication with you and others who can give support, empathy, and guidance in ways to cope better with difficult circumstances. A suicidal fantasy is not a treasured secret. It must be discussed and evaluated. It signifies that a child is desperately trying to cope with inner pain and pressures. Speaking openly with someone who wants to help is a most important way to decrease a child's suicidal tendencies. Such dialogue must be promoted continuously.

When a Child May Have Been Abused

Child abuse, whether physical or sexual, is a complicated and emotion-laden issue. It destroys the child's basic trust in the adult world. Besides feelings of profound distrust, there may also be feelings of intense rage and guilt that can be overwhelming to the child. The child can no longer feel secure and protected, and these feelings of insecurity may also create pervasive feelings of helplessness and hopelessness. There may also be thoughts of being "no good" or "worthless." For example, a child may think, "If my father hates me and hits me, how can anybody like me or see me as good?" Another dilemma for the child may be that if he or she chooses to tell someone, the situation may get worse and punishment may ensue. In working with allegations of child abuse or maltreatment, clinicians must keep themselves attuned to their own feelings, the child's and the family's needs, and other professionals' or agencies' concerns.

Barbara, age 7, was seen by you for an evaluation of suspected sexual and/or physical abuse. The referral was made by Child Protective Services after it received a report from Barbara's mother indicating that Barbara had not been her usual self after having spent the last weekend at her father's house. The mother suspected that Barbara may have been abused. The parents had recently divorced and settled on joint custody of Barbara. A physical examination requested by the mother after the weekend and performed by Barbara's pediatrician was negative except for a bruise on Barbara's arm.

At the first meeting, the mother tells you that Barbara has been sleeping and eating poorly since the weekend at her father's house. She relates to you that Barbara has had nightmares during this time period and has also wet her bed. The mother also tells you that Barbara's schoolteacher was concerned enough to call her because Barbara was acting disinterested in her subjects and seemed to be daydreaming. This is very atypical of Barbara, who is usually very enthusiastic about school. Furthermore, the teacher also reported that there had been some change in Barbara's behavior prior to the weekend in question.

There is much anger in the mother's voice as she speaks to you, and it is not clear whether the anger is due to the present situation or is a residue of the divorce. The mother is concerned that sexual abuse may have occurred, although actual details of the weekend visit are scanty. There are already several individuals and systems involved in this case: lawyers involved with the divorce, a father who is being accused, Child Protective Services, and Barbara and her mother.

Your primary focus at this initial point should be on Barbara and her safety. You tell the mother that you would also like to get from her and from the father further history about the visit, Barbara's background, the family, and the divorce. You also need to see Barbara alone and, if possible, in the presence of each parent. Subsequently, you will write a report to the referring agency.

As noted above, the first goal in this type of situation is to ensure the child's safety. In this case, visitation with the father will have to be temporarily discontinued or held under supervision during the evaluation. Additional goals are to clarify what happened, assess the impact of the event on the child, and begin to assess the background, relationships, motivations, and problem areas of child and/or parents that may have contributed to the suspected abuse.

You interview Barbara's mother and father separately. The story that emerges seems to be that Barbara's mother noted the bruise when Barbara returned from the visit and that Barbara seemed quiet and withdrawn. She questioned Barbara, who responded that "things had gone fine" during the visit. She had bruised herself, she said, when she fell while running after the dog in the yard.

The father initially disclaimed knowledge of the bruise and also thought the visit had gone well for both Barbara and himself. He did say that Barbara had seemed particularly unruly and unmanageable since the divorce, and he had had to physically compel her to sit down and eat or to go upstairs and get ready for bed during recent visits, whereas verbal direction had been sufficient before. Perhaps, he suggested, he had unknowingly bruised her arm when he had held it and told her to remain seated at the dinner table.

Having obtained these differing statements from the parents, you hope that the contact with Barbara will be more illuminating. Your initial emphasis with her is to discover what happened. You introduce yourself and tell her something of what you already know from your contacts with others. Since she has already talked with the protective service worker, it is important to acknowledge your relationship to that person. You might say, for example, "Ms. Jones and I often work together when a boy or girl may have been treated badly or been hurt." It is also important to talk to her about the purpose and agenda of the evaluation.

Although Barbara seems to be attentive to what you are saying, she appears fearful and unwilling to engage in conversation. You ask her about her recent loss of interest in school and her nightmares, but she is reticent and does not elaborate. You acknowledge that this conversation may be upsetting to her and that it is sometimes difficult to talk about problems that may be present in the family. Your goal, you assure her, is to learn what has happened to her recently and to help her and her family.

You sense, however, that Barbara is under considerable stress and is probably conflicted by her divided loyalties to her parents. It is likely that she is afraid of possible rejection by one parent or both. It will take more time to gain her trust and learn more about what happened.

At the next session, you continue to support Barbara and tell her that you understand how hard it is for children to know whether or not to tell something when they are frightened or may have made a promise not to share the information with anyone. She readily agrees to this statement. You then introduce her to your collection of toys and, pointing to your dolls and dollhouse, ask her if it would be easier to show you with the dolls what occurred at her father's house. She seems relieved by this suggestion. She begins to construct a scene in which the girl misbehaves and breaks a chair. The father then hits the girl and throws her onto the couch.

Although upset by the scene she has recreated, Barbara is pleased to have finally "told" someone what occurred. It was much easier for her to use the dolls than to talk about the incident. After further exploration, you feel that the bruise on her arm was the result of an angry outburst by her father. There seems to have been no definite evidence of sexual abuse. A joint session with her and her father indicated generally positive interactions between the two, although she appeared somewhat reticent in his presence.

In this instance, Barbara's play scene seems to have metaphorically expressed violence, or her fear of violence, toward her. The play shows you some of her feelings, but does not necessarily depict actual events. Only by integrating the child's play, joint sessions with her and her parents individually and/or together, and individual sessions with her and other people involved around the time of the event can you formulate a more complete clinical impression.

There are numerous problems in evaluating cases of children in which there are allegations of sexual or physical abuse. One such problem is the need to maintain a focus on the child's emotional and physical needs without overidentifying with the agenda of one parent or another. Another is that of responding appropriately to the legitimate needs of agencies or professionals while also considering the child and parents. A third consists of understanding and effectively managing one's own emotional reactions to physical abuse, sexual abuse, or maltreatment of a child.

The vignette presented above did not provide all the information that a clinician would need about the child and family to fully evaluate the situation. Whether "abuse" has occurred is difficult to determine. In this vignette, Barbara's mother may have wanted to satisfy her own needs—personal and legal—by portraying the father as abusive to the child. Her father may have wanted to indicate that her mother's caretaking abilities were inadequate, as exemplified by Barbara's "misbehavior" and emotional deterioration before and after the event. He may have tried to restrain Barbara in a manner that would not have been called "abusive" prior to the divorce. Barbara's symbolic play indicating possible misbehavior and punishment raises hypotheses about her feelings and about what happened at the weekend visit, but is not conclusive regarding actual events that occurred. Her father's disciplining may or may not have been excessive. Further observation of the situation is warranted, as is therapeutic help for Barbara and her parents in dealing with the divorce and with issues of visitation. At this time, there may not be enough evidence to support a conclusion that child abuse occurred.

A final word in working with child abuse cases. It is often helpful to work with a colleague if at all possible. Consulting with a colleague to help you clarify your understanding of what has been reported to you about the incident, your reactions to it, and your recommendations can be useful. Working jointly with colleagues in the therapy of these difficult cases can also be helpful and provide needed emotional support.

When a Child Threatens to Run Away

The child who runs away is saying that living at home is psychologically intolerable. Such behavior challenges the therapist and other adults to respond immediately with effective action to protect the child and to initiate the process of understanding the child's behavior. The following vignette illustrates some of the problems and challenges in such a situation.

Mark, age 12, is an angry and provocative youngster who often elicits from his parents a reaction in the form of punishment. He has been in treatment with you for approximately one year and trusts and confides in you. He thinks of you as an ally in a hostile world. His presenting problems were school failure, fighting with peers, and several minor stealing episodes. There is also marital disharmony, which upsets and preoccupies him.

One afternoon, Mark shows up at your office unannounced, just as you are leaving to go home. He informs you that he has run away from home, taking $100 that he has been saving to buy a 10-speed bike, and is on the way to the bus station to go across the country. He has come to say goodbye and does not want you to interfere. You are touched by his caring for you and how important a person you are for him. Despite his statement about not wanting you to intervene, you wonder what motivated him to come to your office.

There are several things that have to be done in addition to understanding and responding empathetically to Mark's situation. He should not be allowed to leave your office unattended, even if he must be physically restrained. His safety is paramount. Your own schedule is also secondary. You may have to simply ignore it or, if possible, rearrange it. You will have to inform Mark's parents and perhaps appropriate social agencies.

With these points in mind, you talk to Mark about what has happened. He tells you about the quarrel he has just had with his father. Apparently, Mark has provoked his father because of an incident that prevented him from getting home from school on time. The intensity of anger expressed by his father frightened Mark. He was also angry when his father said he could not go on a weekend trip with his friend and his friend's family because of the incident. He felt this was unfair and impulsively decided to run away.

You listen to Mark's story in a supportive manner and show your concern. You tell him that you are glad he has come to talk with you and that he feels he can confide in you. You also say that running away is not the answer and will not solve his problems with his parents. You would like to work with him and his parents to solve this crisis in a better way. You know that the situation at home has to be worked on and improved. You say that you would like to speak with them and him right away. You say that it would be best if he calls them from your office, but you can call them if he wishes. After a good deal of further discussion and support, Mark agrees, somewhat grudgingly, to a plan of action.

Mark has decided that you should call his parents. You do so and explain to them that Mark is in your office and is alright. They were worried—and angry. They agree to come to your office immediately.

While Mark's parents are on their way, you continue talking to Mark. You do this to provide further support and to make sure Mark's resolve not to run away does not falter, as it might if he were left alone. You are impressed with how quickly Mark is able to calm down when you hear him out patiently. You make a mental note to remind his parents about this characteristic. You realize how strongly Mark yearns to be "heard" and how he has shown himself able to tolerate criticism of his beliefs and actions when others, including his parents, take the time to listen to him.

Before Mark's parents arrive, you consider the best way to approach this difficult situation. You realize that his parents may have numerous reactions to his running away, including anger and frustration with him. They may also have both positive and negative feelings toward you, the person their son has sought out in this crisis. It is also possible that they will expect you to take their side. You will have to assess the situation carefully, including the family's potential for violence, and whether it is safe for Mark to return home. If it is not, Mark may need temporary housing elsewhere. Social service agencies may have to be involved. All this may take several hours. You will not get home for dinner.

The parents finally arrive and, as you expected, are no longer worried, but rather are furious and embarrassed because of Mark's behavior. They also feel that Mark is using you to retaliate against them. It takes a good deal of effort, by talking both with them alone and together with Mark, to convince them that Mark has expressed behavior that is not only unacceptable to them but also an understandable reaction and fear of his own, and that his safety and security must be ensured. You make a strong effort to be supportive to the parents and to learn their point of view. It is important that they, like Mark, feel that you have "heard" them.

It becomes clear during the discussion that Mark's father's anger at Mark is not in adequate control. Fortunately, he can recognize this. There is a favorite aunt of Mark's who lives in the area, and the mother calls her. She agrees to allow Mark to stay with her for at least a month. Mark seems happy at this possibility, since he can continue at the same school. Mark's father and mother agree that a cooling-off period might be helpful.

Plans are made for you to see Mark and his parents the next day. More understanding of the event that brought Mark so unexpectedly to your office, as well as work on how the family deals with problems, is urgently needed if Mark is to return home. A reappraisal of what has happened thus far in your work with Mark and his parents is also in order, and if necessary, a change in therapeutic direction needs to be considered. A question of whether Mark's running away from his parents at this time might partially reflect aspects of his or their reactions to your therapeutic work with him must be considered. Longer term plans for Mark's living situation need to be developed if the home is not safe and secure for him after this crisis intervention.

Although a cold dinner awaits you, there is some satisfaction in knowing that you have handled the crisis well. Mark and his parents both feel that they have been heard; the alliance they have with you seems to have been strengthened by the crisis. Mark's safety has been ensured. Support has been marshaled for him, and both his parents and he agree to more intensive therapeutic work on the problems from which he had tried to "run away."

DIFFICULT MOMENTS INVOLVING THE FREEDOMS AND LIMITS IN PSYCHOTHERAPY

When a Child Steals from Your Office

Play objects are very important to children and may take on symbolic meanings beyond their use as articles of enjoyment. Toys in a playroom offer particular temptations to children. Sometimes, children are tempted simply because they have few toys at home. At other times, their desire to take toys or other objects from the playroom or waiting area reflects other, more internal needs as well. It is not uncommon for a child to "steal" play objects or other materials from the therapist's office or waiting area. Some aspects of the management of these instances are indicated in the following vignette.

Barry, an 8-year-old, has been seen by you in therapy for two months. He rapidly formed a therapeutic relationship with you. While playing with cars and trucks in your office, the two of you have been talking about problems at home that center around Barry's relationship with his father. A session with Barry earlier that day had gone particularly well, but then, three patients later, and well into the afternoon, you learn of a missing car when John, another patient, exclaims, "There's an orange car missing from this box!"

When a later search under the desk, behind the chair, and on the various shelves does not uncover the missing car, you find yourself reasoning that Barry almost certainly took it. In today's session, while playing with the car, he had said how much he liked it and wished he had one like it at home. Also, you realize that the two girls you had seen after Barry on this day had shown no interest in cars, preferring dolls and board games.

There is a question of what to do. After all, you really did not see Barry take the car and you do not want to falsely accuse him. You could decide to avoid a confrontation at this time and hope that if Barry did take the car, it was an isolated incident, the meaning and importance of which can be understood and dealt with later in the therapy. A better solution and one that at least acknowledges that something is missing would be to see if Barry brings up the car in the next session and, if he does not, mentioning its loss and your concern about it. Then, if a second car is taken at a later session and it is again clear that Barry has taken it, you would directly voice your concerns to Barry and ask him if he knew what had happened to the car. Depending on his response, you would remind him of the first incident and point out the circumstances making you suspect that he might have taken both cars.

In this illustration, during the next session, as you and Barry are again playing with trucks and cars, you notice an orange car slipping out of his pants pocket. Red faced, Barry picks up the orange car and puts it on the table in the line up of other cars and trucks, thereby thwarting your initial wish to avoid an immediate confrontation that you feared might disturb the positive relationship with Barry. Perhaps, in retrospect, there was in the wish too much of your own desire to avoid a "confrontation" anyway.

It is important to think of the symbolic meaning of taking the car, but you also have to deal directly with the situation at hand. "Barry," you say, "this looks like a car we played with last time. I thought it was missing after the last session we had."

Barry's red face is downcast, but he says nothing.

You continue, "It seems you took the car out of the playroom. I think it is important for us to talk about why that happened."

He still sits quietly.

You try to convey to him that you understand he may be feeling bad because you found out he took the car from the playroom, and it may be hard to talk about. Later, when this discussion is not productive, you also suggest some confusion on your part. You question why he brought the car back to the session: Was it because of guilt, fear of discovery, or what? Probing of these possibilities is also to no avail, however, and Barry simply says, in pathetic denial, "I just found it outside the room."

It seems that this event will be talked about in its symbolic context much more, but you feel it is still necessary to state certain rules of the therapy. You could say something like this: "Barry, I know that having a car that we have used together is important to you, but I want to reemphasize three essential rules of our working together: There is no hitting or fighting in our sessions, there is no intentional breaking of anything, and there is no taking anything that isn't yours."

That should be enough said for the first time. At some

later date, if the stealing continues, you could of course speak further with Barry's parents about the stealing and work with them and with him to try and understand its meaning in the context of the sessions. Careful assessment of whether there is stealing or other conduct problems outside the sessions would also be crucial. Some therapists would also consider countering the stealing behavior with behavioral procedures such as a response cost. Supervision of Barry in the waiting area would also help to set limits on his behavior as you make it clear to him that this added supervision will give the two of you time to understand his stealing without having to stop the sessions.

Finally, if there continues to be "stealing" in the therapy setting, there is a good chance Barry is stealing elsewhere, too, and may have a number of other conduct problems. You might then emphasize to Barry that he seems to be showing you, by his actions, that it is necessary to consider the possibility of other therapy settings or placements outside the home, where he could get more supervision and treatment. Usually, things do not get this far and this latter discussion will not be needed.

It must be emphasized that the particular symbolic and communicative intentions of the stealing have to be worked out in the therapy with the individual child. Barry, for example, may be "stealing" to symbolically gain an object that he feels unworthy of having or receiving because of who he is as a person. He may be trying to increase his personal, symbolic value by taking the car because doing so seems to make him older, stronger, more powerful, more independent, or more active than he now feels himself to be. He may also be saying that he has so little trust in his own worthiness to have others give to him or satisfy his needs, as well as so little confidence that others will see, know, or care about his needs, that he must secretly satisfy his own needs, for no one else will.

There are other possibilities as well. He may be testing the reaction of others to the taking of their possessions to see whether he or the possessions mean more to them. He may be trying to determine how far others will let his actions go before calling a halt. He may be trying to gain attention by being punished, and being known as someone special to you, even if it is as a negative figure, rather than feeling lost or insignificant among your other patients.

The unraveling of all these possibilities is the process and work of therapy. It occurs within the context of a particular structure and established rules and often proceeds partly by suggesting hypotheses and possibilities to the child and to yourself, based on his or her history, play, or interactions with you in the sessions. With Barry, as you "lay down the law" to him about stealing not being allowed, you also begin the process of understanding the stealing behavior, by, for example, commenting that it seems that having a car from the playroom was very important to him and you "wonder" why that is. Additional later comments such as, "That orange car is something that we've played with a lot here together," may also open up avenues to approach dynamic meanings, as might comments such as, "I wonder what you might have done with the car if you had kept it at home?"

When a Child Is Aggressive toward You

One of the most difficult problems with which child psychotherapist may be faced is how to deal with a child who is aggressive or out of control during a session. Such circumstances may escalate to produce an immediately dangerous circumstance, and they require quick thinking and action by the therapist. The following vignette highlights intervention strategies that can be considered and used.

Finger Painter, at the age of 8, was notorious at school. A

brilliant child academically, he was considered to be the "Dennis the Menace" of his third-grade class. Since kindergarten, he had been renowned for his unpredictable mischievous actions, among the more notable of which were throwing blocks at teachers in kindergarten, tearing books in the first grade, pulling girls' hair in the second grade, and jumping from desk to desk in the third grade. Perplexed about this repetitious trend in his behavior, his parents sought a psychiatric consultation from you after several neurological evaluations had shown no organic cause for his impulsive and aggressive actions.

During the initial discussion with the parents, you learn that Finger Painter has shown signs of unpredictability since the age of 4, when his sister was born. On some days, he did not want to attend nursery school and had lengthy temper tantrums. Usually, however, he went to nursery school with enthusiasm. His teachers, too, observed frequent episodes of irritability, oppositionalism, and impulsivity.

Finger Painter's parents report that he is reluctant to see you. However, he finally acquiesced after his parents promised to buy him a toy he had been asking for. At the first meeting, he walks with you to your office and watches intently as you enter the room. He finds a seat and waits silently to see what will happen next.

You introduce yourself and try to engage him in a discussion about why he is here. You tell him that his parents came to speak with you because they wondered why there were problems at school.

Finger Painter listens and tells you that he did not want to come to see you, but his parents insisted. Although he is very verbal, he seems angry and reluctant to converse. You show him where the toys are and suggest that he may want to use them while you talk with him. Appearing to appreciate this suggestion, Finger Painter begins to inspect the variety of

playthings. He comments on the selection of toys and especially notes that he has some of them at home. It appears that he is becoming more comfortable in the meeting and is slowly becoming engaged in interactions with you. He certainly is an appealing child, and you begin to wonder if the difficulties described by his parents are exaggerated. But wait—premature conclusions sometimes precede difficult moments.

Finger Painter points out that he likes to draw and tells you about a paint set with many colors that his parents promised to buy for him. This spontaneously volunteered information is encouraging to you. When he suggests that he would like to paint a picture, you feel triumphant and are tempted to conclude that you have created a working alliance with him. Finger Painter even suggests that you, too, paint a picture. You feel exhilarated that he not only wants to play, but also is willing to involve you!

Finger Painter finds several jars of paint and appears gleeful. Carefully, he begins to work with you to prepare a place at the table large enough for you to make a "big painting." He smiles as he quickly opens the jars of red, yellow, green, blue, and black paint. He looks up at you and smiles again as he hands you a paintbrush. He seems to be solicitous of your needs and encourages you to sit down at the table and paint with him.

Finger Painter uses broad, rapid strokes to execute his own painting. He appears to be intensely involved and very excited. Meanwhile, you begin to paint your own picture. Suddenly, Finger Painter seems to be more out of control. He begins to splatter large gobs of paint all over his paper. You realize that you may be observing the type of problem behavior discussed by his parents. This is the "gold" of the therapeutic process—to have an opportunity to observe how a symptom develops and is expressed!

Until this point, Finger Painter has been using a brush and making long, wide strokes. However, he drops the brush and begins to smear paint with his fingers and palms. His movements become very rapid. You become concerned that he may be out of control. What should you do?

There are several options.

You recognize that limits need to be set. You try to structure this situation and establish control. You ask Finger Painter what he is painting, hoping that by distracting him and intervening verbally you will decrease his impulsivity and diminish the out-of-control behavior. You also try to gain his interest and establish interpersonal contact by asking about the picture. All to no avail. Such interventions frequently work with children who are carried away by their own actions. However, this is not the case with Finger Painter. He smears on. The paint is beginning to slop off the paper and onto the table!

You perhaps try the next option, momentarily forgetting your enthusiasm for witnessing the "gold" of the therapeutic process. You tell Finger Painter that he seems to be getting overexcited about his painting and that he needs to gain more control before he can continue. Perhaps a rest from his activity would help. You say clearly, calmly, and directly that you both should stop painting now. He will be able to finish his painting at another time. The two of you will work together to clean his hands and the tabletop.

Fond hope—things have gone too far! Finger Painter apparently interprets your limits as a criticism, deprivation, or implicit attack. He responds without warning by hitting you with both open hands. You are shocked! He has not only hit you, but also smeared two blue handprints on your yellow sweater. Finger Painter, too, seems shocked and suddenly sits down with a surprised and frightened look on his face. It is as if he, too, wonders how far he will go.

At least the violence has stopped. Had it continued, you would have had to restrain him physically and hold him until he regained control. Working in an area in which there are other people who might be available to help can be important if you alone cannot impose adequate restraint.

"What now?," you wonder. You feel like a victim of child violence. Certainly you have experienced and observed the evolution of your patient's symptom, but was this necessary to help you understand your patient? Was it worth it?

In a quieter moment, you realize that you have shared similar reactions that others have had when Finger Painter was in their midst. You feel shocked, disappointed, betrayed, angry, mistrustful,—and also a bit empathic with his forlorn-appearing state. But, how to respond? The following are possible responses:

One way of dealing with the situation is to express your feelings directly as long as you remember to take Finger Painter's therapeutic needs into consideration. You could then say his behavior has made you angry and is not tolerable. You will have to take the paints away and terminate the session, since he will have to gain more control of himself and you will have to clean your sweater and the room. Next time, you would like to discuss what happened with him. These responses express realistically human feelings. They may be helpful, but remember not to appear out of control in your remarks.

Another approach is to remain calm and control your intense feelings. You may explain to Finger Painter that there are limits to what is acceptable behavior in the meetings with you. You can tell him that anything can be discussed, but no one is to get hurt and certain behaviors are not allowed. To emphasize these rules, you should tell him that he has lost control of his behavior while painting and that the paints must be put away. You can suggest that you both get cleaned up and state that until he can demonstrate better control, painting during the sessions will not be possible.

Having followed one of these courses of actions, you may wish to continue the session and discuss how this type of out-of-control behavior may be similar to that described by other people who know him. The value of these approaches is that they provide you with an opportunity to evaluate his feelings regarding the impact of his behaviors. Does he feel sorry, can he gain control, does he blame you for causing this behavior, does he feel sad?

Given the degree of aggression and impulsivity that Finger Painter has shown, it seems wise to discuss what happened and include his parents and him at the end of the session. The purpose of this tactic is to allow the entire family to recognize that a significant problem exists, that therapeutic intervention is needed, and that you will be working with them to understand the problem and develop ways to deal with it. This discussion should also be aimed at discouraging the possibility of Finger Painter's parents being angry with him and punishing him for the events in the session. On the other hand, they certainly have to know about the degree of his problems. You want to impart the message that this behavior is not acceptable, but that he, his family, and you will work together to help with the problems.

A number of other issues are also highlighted by this vignette. Should you hold the family responsible for damage to your clothes? This raises a broader issue about what is an appropriate reaction when a child's actions result in damages to your office. A sanguine approach is to evaluate the extent of damage. For example, damage to furniture or windows may be appropriate items for family responsibility. Of course, damage to toys is inevitable and is to be expected as a common occurrence.

What kind of play objects are most effective as facilitators of expressive psychotherapy? A common adage is that any type of toy that is not dangerous is acceptable. Toys that are most valuable are those that stimulate fantasy, such as dolls, puppets, and crayons. A word of caution about paints, clay, and sand. These and other materials for the visual arts are good for provoking fantasy, but their use often lessens behavioral controls. Many children demonstrate regressed behaviors when working with them. Therefore, be prepared to have to deal with occasional episodes similar to the one with Finger Painter just described! Remember that to be a child therapist means to be at risk of such occupational hazards as being soiled, spat on, hit, and kicked.

When a Child Is Sexually Provocative in Therapy

Psychotherapy is the process of self-disclosure. The goals are to explore problematic emotions and behaviors and to help develop realistic changes. In a sense, the patient who enters psychotherapy agrees to be in a situation in which genuine openness, honesty, trust, and cooperation are key ingredients in the process of treatment. Some children may conceptualize these views so concretely that during therapy they engage in behaviors that are provocative and inappropriate even in that setting. A psychotherapist for children will invariably encounter situations such as that illustrated by the following example.

Billy, age 7, began treatment with you because he has had great difficulty making friends and prefers to be alone. Initially, he was shy with you. He spoke little and appeared to be intensely observant of your actions. Soon, however, Billy became more relaxed and animated. He now looks forward to seeing you and enthusiastically uses your toys and also brings his own toys to the session. He acknowledges that he feels more comfortable with peers since coming to see you

and that he likes to talk with you. He has imaginative, creative, and vivid fantasies during play. There is little evidence of shyness or inhibition as he rapidly comes to view you as a special person in his life.

One day, Billy comes into the session and quickly puts his book bag down, takes off his coat, and then...proceeds to undress. You watch him with great surprise! A number of thoughts immediately race through your mind. Should you stop him? What should you say? You feel confused, embarrassed, and even shy. You remember that you are a doctor who has seen many children undressed. You remember that as a child psychotherapist, you should be prepared for almost any type of remark and behavior. Yet this is the first time that you have been in this type of situation!

As these thoughts race through your mind, you partly decide not to be impulsive and you partly cannot decide what to do, and so you continue to observe what Billy is doing. You try quickly to understand what he wishes to accomplish by disrobing in your office.

First, you consider possible meanings for this behavior and wonder if he is being exhibitionistic and if so why. Has he become so uninhibited with you that he bizarrely wants you to know him in all aspects? Has he been sexually excited in the sessions and does he now feel comfortable enough with you to offer or allow explicit sexual activity?

As these thoughts occur, you continue to observe Billy's behavior. He has already taken off his shoes and socks, his shirt is next, and now he unzips his pants. Casually, then, without excitement, he pulls his pants off. He has on a T-shirt and a pair of shorts, which seem to be a part of a school sports outfit. As he takes a pair of running shoes out of his book bag and begins to put them on, he invites you to play with the sponge ball in the toy cabinet and proudly shows you his school's logo on the T-shirt. He has obviously made the track team!

In response to your relieved and stunned look, Billy denies that he wants to show you his social accomplishment and informs you that he does not want to mess up his school clothes and prefers to play in his team outfit. He does not elaborate further, and you decide not to question him more at this time. Although his self-confidence and bravado in front of you, along with taking off his clothes, may have some sexual meaning, clearly his actions do not constitute overt sexual provocation. He is feeling much less inhibited with you and wants to share his accomplishments openly with you.

Yet other children, more disturbed than Billy, may begin to disrobe, ask the therapist to disrobe, touch the therapist's breasts or genitals, ask the therapist to touch their breasts or genitals, or otherwise act in direct sexual provocation. Consider the situation with another child, Johnny. He is a 5-year-old who has been sexually abused in at least one of the day-care programs in which his drug-abusing mother placed him. He initially seemed reluctant to come alone to a therapy session with his female therapist. In the first four sessions, however, his play was appropriate and he was interested in throwing balls, using Play Doh to make animal forms, and exploring a set of cars and trucks in the room. By the third session, he became interested in the dollhouse and the figures in it. He squealed and smiled anxiously when he put boy and girl dolls together in bed. It nevertheless took the therapist by surprise when he got up from the floor, seemingly to get another doll from the toy cabinet, and instead approached the therapist, touched her breast, and asked excitedly, "Do you want to touch my pee pee?"

This situation required empathy, support, and firm limits. The therapist calmly took Johnny's hand off her breast and said: "There is no touching of one another in our sessions. It seems like grown-ups may have touched you on your pee pee before and may have wanted you to touch them on their breasts or on their pee pee. I think that doing those things may make you nervous and is not right between adults and children. In our sessions, we should try and understand whether the fighting and nervousness and running away that have been problems for you over the last few months have to do with scary behavior like that which may be confusing and frightening to you." Later, she added: "In our sessions, it is good to talk about what you feel, or what has happened before. Sometimes it is easier to show what has happened or what you think about by using dolls, Play Doh, drawings or whatever you would like. Without you actually touching me, or me touching you, our sessions will be less scary, and we will still be able to work on your problems."

A child's sexually provocative behavior can be one of the more challenging and anxiety-provoking situations in psychotherapeutic work with children. Although it is essential that you maintain an observant approach, it is also mandatory that you have sufficient control of the situation to ensure that the child learns appropriate behavioral limits during the therapy session. In the case of Billy, there was no indication (after a period of uncertainty entirely on your part!) that he was going to do any more than partially disrobe. However, a child like Johnny might have attempted to run out of the room while naked or to engage you in sexual behavior. If such things occur in the session, you should initiate discussion between you and the child about what happened, as well as institute appropriate controls on the actual behavior. You should also explore the meaning of the child's problematic behavior with the parents as part of your session with them. In some ways, this approach is similar to the one used if a child engages in other types of out-of-control behaviors that may be harmful to him or her or to others. The important things to remember are that the child's behavior reflects his or her internal needs or conflicts and perhaps his or her expectations of what adults want or will reward. Clear limits are needed so that exploration, understanding, and working through the child's reactions are possible. Sometimes a child will find it so sexually stimulating to be with a therapist who is psychologically identified with the perpetrator of the sexual abuse that individual sessions are not possible, at least initially. An example of this might be a sexually abused girl who cannot be alone in a playroom with a young male therapist. It may be necessary in some cases, at least initially, for therapy sessions to take place in a more open space such as a playground area or in the company of another adult who is not identified with the perpetrator, or even to be conducted by a different therapist.

DIFFICULT MOMENTS INVOLVING THE TIME, PLACE, AND STRUCTURE OF PSYCHOTHERAPY

When a Child Invites You to Celebrate a Special Occasion

Birthdays, graduations, bar mitzvahs, bas mitzvahs, and confirmations are milestones in most children's lives. The pleasure and self-esteem that are derived from such occasions are usually lasting memories for a child. All children like to celebrate special events, and they usually wish to have people who are important to them participate in their celebration. It is inevitable, therefore, that such occasions become the focus of special attention during psychotherapy sessions. In fact, these events require such additional attention simply because they are unique and special to the child. Nevertheless, children react to these life events in different ways. The example of one child will illustrate general principles that require consideration for psychotherapeutic management when children invite a therapist to share an event with them outside the therapeutic setting.

Amy is a severely learning-disabled girl almost 13 years old who has been in treatment with you for 2 years. She entered treatment because she was withdrawn, not getting along with classmates, shy, anxious, and sad. Notably, Amy felt inept and negative about herself. In social situations, she did not know how to respond, especially with peers. She was very serious and spoke so deliberately that her peers teased her excessively. In the last three years, she has been attending a school for learning-disabled children.

During the course of her 2-year treatment with you, many of her symptoms have diminished. Amy is more confident and able to understand her problems with peers. Her academic performance has improved, and she likes attending classes. Amy is exceptionally attached to you. She values your ideas and suggestions. Most of all, she considers you to be her special and trusted friend who gives her good advice. She believes that you help her to be happy, hopeful, and more adventurous.

Amy's bas mitzvah is scheduled to take place in three months. Her parents have made special arrangements with the rabbi, who will practice intensively with Amy so that she can read from the Bible without being overwhelmed by her learning problems. In one of her therapy sessions, Amy invites you to her bas mitzvah, explaining that she will be less nervous and better able to read from the Bible if you are there.

Amy's invitation to attend her bas mitzvah was not a surprise. You realize that she very much wants you to come

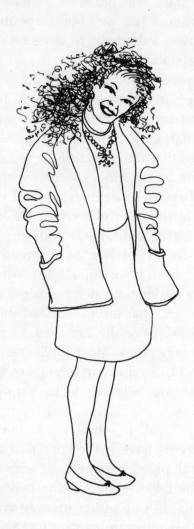

and wants a quick answer, but you also realize that an essential task of managing her invitation is to explore her fantasies of and motivations for the invitation. You tell her that you appreciate and are happy to receive her invitation and will consider whether you will go to her bas mitzvah. You choose not to give a definite yes or no at this time.

Although you would like to share the event with Amy, there are several issues to consider with regard to attending. Sharing an event with Amy outside the therapy room may change the treatment relationship you have with her. Once you are a part of her social life, she may have more difficulty in talking about her problems in this area or may feel embarrassed by her difficulties and reticent to discuss them with you, as has been the case between her and her parents. She may feel enthusiastic about your coming, and in her imaginings she may feel that she has to attend to you or please you so much at the social event that her expected relationships with others will be distorted. If you go to this event and it works out well, she may expect you to come to future events and to provide the support she may also need at those times. Although the bas mitzvah may seem at this moment in her life to be an event of importance never to be exceeded, a graduation may seem equally important later on. You will then have to explain why you came to one event and not the other. Not going would also cause Amy to have a number of reactions. She may feel angry at you and may not understand your explanation. She may think that you do not like her or are not concerned about her.

On the other hand, your coming to the bas mitzvah and showing support for Amy's needs at this special time may show her in a concrete way that you value her, her needs, and her ideas of what is important. In large measure, she often feels that these concerns of hers have been neglected in the past. That you, her special person, would come to her memorable event may give her self-esteem a great boost and allow additional trust in you.

There is no easy answer. A crucial additional variable is how you feel. What is your schedule like? If you attend Amy's bas mitzvah, will you be committing yourself to attending other children's ceremonies? For example, you realize that you have other patients from the same community. Do you feel comfortable in expanding the boundaries of the therapy session? Some therapists prefer to deal with their patients only within the therapy setting. They do not wish to have the spotlight on them out of that setting. Like many other professional people, they quite understandably do not want to have to be "professionals" outside business hours. Other therapists enjoy social occasions, bas mitzvahs, graduations, and the chance to get to know their patients in a broader context. Moreover, their doing so sometimes helps in the therapy.

In Amy's case, you decide not to go. This decision is based on your concern that a blurring of the boundaries between Amy's therapeutic world, family world, and social world would be confusing to her. She has already become strongly attached to you in the therapy sessions, and you have sensed that her mother may feel some competition with you. You are concerned that Amy's attention to you outside the session will make you "larger than life" and in this way distort your therapeutic relationship with her. You tell Amy that you are very excited about the event and feel glad that she will share it with her family and friends. You explain to her that your relationship with her is unique and involves trying to understand how she feels and responds to people and events like her bas mitzvah. You can help her most not by going to her bas mitzvah, but by having her discuss her ideas and feelings about it with you. Perhaps she would like to show you pictures taken at the ceremony during a subsequent session.

Once you have made your decision, you recognize that the most important therapeutic task is to further explore with Amy the meaning of the bas mitzvah and of your decision. In this way, you hope to help her prepare for the event, cope with conflicts about it, and gain more understanding about your relationship with her.

One of the things Amy wishes to discuss in the therapy, which you think may have been an aspect of her invitation to you, is emphasized when she tells you that she is worried that her guests will not have a good time. She feels responsible for them and, because she is socially insecure, believes that they will be critical of her and not enjoy her special day. You decide to focus on how she perceives her role as a good hostess at the bas mitzvah. You help her to realize that although she should respond cordially, she should not consider herself entirely responsible for her guests' feelings and behaviors. You help her to see that her guests need to take care of themselves and that they will enjoy themselves if she is relaxed. You also ask her if she has thought about discussing plans for entertainment of the guests with her mother and whether planning this with her mother might occur. You make a mental note to talk about the bas mitzvah with Amy's mother during the next scheduled visit with her. Amy understands these suggestions and seems to be relieved that she can concentrate more on her own feelings and actions. She looks forward to being a gracious hostess.

Although Amy does not raise the subject, you realize that it may be helpful for her to discuss the thoughts she has about the Bible reading. You are cognizant of her learning disabilities and suspect that she is also. Does she feel confident, or is she anxious about learning her part and reciting it at her bas mitzvah? In discussions, the two of you work out a plan for her to practice at specific times during the day. Ulti-mately, Amy tells you that she feels enthusiastic and that she will be able to learn her part. She suggests that she would like to read her part to you prior to the event. You are eager to hear her Bible reading and share your pleasure with her. With these major problems dealt with, Amy can have much more fun thinking about friends to invite, foods to have at the reception, and decorating the room in which the party will be held.

This example highlights several important principles re-garding a child's invitation to a therapist to attend a special event. Amy was very striking because of her severe learning disabilities and social awkwardness. It may therefore have seemed that it would have been especially helpful for the therapist to attend the ceremony. However, it should be rec-ognized that special events are uniquely meaningful to every-one. The significance of an event and whether the therapist should attend the ceremony may be related to a host of fac-tors including the child's personality, the therapeutic rela-tionship, and the type and time of the event. For example, a graduation from elementary school may have more of an im-pact than a bar mitzvah occurring in the same year. With regard to the therapeutic process, it is less important that the therapist be present at the event than that there be a complete discussion and understanding of the meaning of the event and of the therapist's participation in it. In the process of the discussion, the child develops insight that should be useful for future events and relationships.

It is accepted that special events not only are memorable but also may have anniversary effects, which can be positive, negative, or both. An important event may have a major impact on future behaviors, feelings, and attitudes toward life situations. It is expected that the psychotherapeutically accrued insights relevant to particular events will significantly affect both the child's future and his or her ability to benefit from other important life events.

When a Child Does Not Want to End the Session

There are many children who crave the special adult attention that a therapeutic relationship provides and in consequence sometimes do not want to end their sessions at the scheduled time. These children can be found lingering around the office area after a session is over, attempting to begin a new game minutes before the therapy session is to end, or overtly or subtly refusing to leave the session. They often tend to seek out extra minutes with their therapist, who may be in a quandary as to whether to continue in what is probably an enjoyable interchange or to set limits on this obvious manipulation of the therapist's time, fearing that such limits may create anger or resentment in the child and possibly retard therapeutic progress. Many therapists tend to acquiesce to these "requests" for added time and quickly get behind in their schedules.

Ann, age 8, has been referred to you due to her oppositional and manipulative behavior. Her parents and teachers view her as being rather precocious and "adultlike" in her verbal skills and in one-to-one child–adult interactions, but excessively demanding and competitive in peer relationships. She tends to fabricate stories and denies any wrongdoing. She blames others for her misdeeds, thus leaving herself without close friends. She attempts to gain the favor of adults, who are often struck by her cuteness and pseudomature behavior.

This is an early session with Ann. She has been quite interactive with you, discussing many of her problems and talking about her relationship with her mother and younger sibling. When you tell Ann that your time with her is up, however, she becomes distressed, her mouth drops, and she becomes quiet for a moment and then more active again. Then, with a new burst of energy, she begins to explore other games in your office.

You try without much success to remind Ann that she has worked hard during the hour, but now the time is up and you will see her next week at the same time. She remains unmoved by your words, however. It is as her mother has said about her "like talking to a wall." She lingers on, apparently not paying attention to your suggestions. You are now quite aware of what her parents and teachers complain about, as your thoughts turn to the family you are scheduled to meet with in ten minutes. Still, you do not want to be insensitive to Ann's increasingly apparent need to hold on to you longer, as expressed by her refusal to leave the session.

Yet, despite your repeated assurances that the two of you will pick up where you left off when you meet again next week, and your reminder that her mother must be waiting for her, Ann continues to delay and opens a new can of Play-Doh. You now begin to have some impatience with her for not responding to your statements aimed at ending the session. Despite what you feel must be your own very noticeable frustration, however, she continues to delay and remains firmly in her chair.

Now, you wonder, "What should I do?" You have tried verbally to suggest that she leave the room several times, with no success. Fantasies abound at times like this. Should you go tell her parents that the session is over and that they can come to your office and pick up their daughter any time? Should you track down your supervisor to tell him that this 8-year-old girl is bullying you? Should you hide in a colleague's office and hope Ann takes the hint?

Finally, you decide on a plan. You want to continue to be sensitive to Ann's feeling of not wanting to go, but at the same time you want to convey to her a nonnegotiable stance.

You decide to reflect to Ann what you think may be some of the reasons for her refusal to leave the session while also setting the practical and necessary limits of the therapy. You say something like this: "Ann, I know it is hard to leave when we have been enjoying our time together and getting to know one another, but the session is over for today. We will see each other again next week."

If there is no response, you might try to help provide a transition for Ann by encouraging her to take home to look at during the week a picture she drew during the session. Alternatively, you could encourage her to write a story or draw a picture that she might want to show you or talk about next time. For most children, a sympathetic acknowledgment of their need to continue being with you, coupled with firmness about the limits of the therapy session, will suffice. In Ann's case, it does not; she continues to twirl back and forth in her chair.

At this point, you stand up, move to the door, and open it so she can leave. You try to convey a sense of expectation that she will comply. If this does not work, tell her that you are going to leave the room now, too, and start out, leaving the door open. In most cases, the child will leave as soon as you do and proceed to the waiting area to find the parents.

Finally, since Ann is an especially difficult child in this situation, and these procedures do not work, you continue to the waiting area yourself and explain briefly to her parents that Ann is demonstrating for you what they have also experienced: difficulty giving up adult attention and doing what others expect of her when these requests do not satisfy her needs at that time. You suggest to them that you all go back to the therapy room and spend a few minutes talking about this with Ann before they take her home. Then, depending on the remaining time available for discussion, clarify for Ann and her parents what has happened at the end of the session.

Tell them that in some ways, it is fortunate that this difficult moment occurred so that you can all understand it better and work on it further in the therapy sessions, which Ann has begun to do already.

At this point after this brief discussion, say that the time is over and you will see them next week. Usually, with parents present, the child will leave without further difficulty. If not, you may have to encourage the parents to escort the child out of the room and, in extreme cases, carry the child away. These measures, of course, should be taken only after you have stated directly to the child and the parents that this is the only recourse if the child is unable to leave without being forced. Sometimes, further encouragement, a light remark, or brief mention of an enjoyable activity that has already been planned for later that day (for example, a visit to a friend's house) is helpful in allowing the child to leave on a positive note without these extreme measures being taken.

When a Child Must Experience a Sudden Interruption in Therapy

Unexpected interruptions in therapy are sometimes unavoidable. They can signify severe loss for the child and family. Issues of abandonment, trust, control, and confidence in the predictability of others may all become apparent. The therapist must be aware of the possibility of severe disruptive and regressive reactions on the part of the child during these times. All this must be managed therapeutically while the therapist is adjusting to new circumstances in his or her own life, including personal and professional losses as well as new opportunities. The following vignette illustrates some of these points.

Billy, age 7, has been attending psychotherapy twice a week for the past 3 months. He was referred to you because

of disruptive behavior both at home and at school. He presented with a variety of psychosomatic complaints and had
been having nightmares, loss of sleep, and irritability. In
school, he had been inattentive and restless and had started
fighting with his peers. The onest of these symptoms occurred soon after his parents' separation, which had occurred
suddenly. The father left the family, apparently abandoning
his wife and Billy to move to another part of the country.

During the initial stages of the therapy, you have provided a sense of constancy and stability for Billy, and the
sessions have been a safe place for him to express his intense
and angry feelings about his father and the family's dissolu-
tion. It has been gratifying for you to work with Billy over
these 3 months and to be able to provide this sense of stability
for him. When you receive a call from a senior colleague
inviting you to be a replacement speaker at a national conference that is to begin the following week, you accept the
invitation, but you realize that this unexpected disruption
will be difficult for all your patients, but especially for Billy.

You start the next session by informing Billy that you will
be gone for the next two weeks and that you will have to miss
the sessions with him. This news startles Billy to a degree that
you had not anticipated. He starts yelling at you and screams
that he hates you and everyone. In tears, he stomps around
the room, agitated and very distraught.

Billy's outburst shows you in a dramatic way how important you have become to him and how great a blow his father's absence has been. You begin to feel guilty for having
intruded disruption and abandonment into his life a second
time. Wanting to calm Billy, and to assure him that you understand his feelings and that you also feel bad that this interruption must occur now, you say: "Billy, I'm sorry that I have
to leave so suddenly and miss our next two sessions. I realize
that my telling you this so soon before I'll be away is upset-

ting and that you are angry. Let's talk about how it will be for you when I'm away."

"I don't want to," Billy retorts angrily. "I don't want to talk to you and I don't ever want to see you again."

"Billy, I had no intention of hurting you, and I apologize if I have, but I needed to share this news with you. I also want to discuss how the two weeks while I'm away will be for you."

"Why should we?," he asks. "You don't care!"

"I know that our work in therapy has been important and we'll both miss seeing each other," you reply.

"I hate you!" is Billy's answer as he still seems unable to accept your leaving.

"Well, I don't hate you. I care a lot about you," you say, trying to reassure him. You realize that he needs a great deal of your concern at this point and also needs to feel sure that you will return and be there to see him again.

It takes the better part of half an hour for Billy's angry outbursts and sobbing to stop and for him to be able to hear your repeated assurances. As you observe him gradually becoming less agitated, you make a mental note of the need to explore further details about his father's leaving. You realize the extent of his suffering much better than previously.

You also remember other patients who have felt somehow responsible when parental separations have occurred. You realize that you will have to further explore with Billy his feelings toward himself. Children in this situation often feel that they are "no good," since important people in their lives have left them without adequate explanation, causing them to wonder if they were at fault.

When Billy becomes calm enough to discuss your upcoming absence, you talk with him about several subjects. These include what he will be doing during the 2 weeks when there will be no sessions, what problems he thinks may come up.during this time, and how he will actually spend the usual hour of the session next week. You tell him, as well as his mother, that a therapist will be covering your patients for emergencies in your absence, and you give him and his mother the therapist's name and telephone number. You also talk with him about how progress can be made even during this interruption in therapy by such strategies as keeping notes of what occurs, making drawings illustrating how he is feeling, or making an audio tape describing what has been happening in his life and what he is thinking. In some cases, depending on the child's needs, it may helpful to send the child a note or a card or make a brief phone call while you are away.

It should be apparent from the foregoing that all interruptions in therapy should be planned if at all possible and discussed at some length in advance. Sometimes it is helpful to clarify at the beginning of therapy that some interruptions are inevitable and cannot always be foreseen. A reassuring statement to parents and child about coverage always being available during your absence may be helpful. In this way, you let the parents and child know that you understand that separation and changes of routine can be very difficult.

For some children, depending on age and cognitive ability, your upcoming vacation times or holidays can be noted on a calendar, with an indication of the sessions that will be missed and their times. This strategy shows the child, in a concrete way, how many sessions you will be missing and when the two of you will be getting back together. It underlines the significance of the relationship to the child. In the vignette, it might have been helpful, after Billy had settled down, to show him a calendar and the date the sessions would resume.

These methods usually reduce the tension and uncertainties that separation, even temporary ones, can produce.

The emphasis is on planning, support as needed, and providing a sense of continuity in the therapeutic relationship.

When a Child Is Anxious about Your Wanting to Contact the School

Psychotherapy is a situation involving, among other things, privacy and a sharing of secret fears, wishes, and disappointments between therapist and child. At times, it is necessary to relay information obtained during psychotherapy sessions to outsiders and to receive information about a child from others in his or her life. Understandably, discussing a child with others can create anxiety for both the child and the family and can result in a questioning of the child's or family's trust or confidence in the therapist, even when permission to talk about the child's or family's problems has been given. The following vignette illustrates a child's reactions to the therapist's saying that a contact with the child's teacher would be desirable.

Bruce, age 9, is an intelligent boy who attends a public school in the area. He has had cerebral palsy since birth. With extensive physical therapy and hard work on his part, his physical disability is now mainly a slight left-sided awkwardness of gait. He is also learning-disabled and has worked hard to overcome his perceptual-motor difficulties. Bruce has no apparent problems in the home environment, where his parents find him to be a pleasant, cheerful, and enthusiastic child. They have adjusted well to his mild disability, at times feeling slightly sad for him because he cannot go on hikes or run as well as the other boys on the block.

Bruce's problems are mainly at school. His third-grade teacher has reported to the parents that he has behavior problems and is excessively shy. He does not speak up in class even when he seems to know the answer. He has gotten into fights with the other boys on the playground and at times is seen cursing and yelling at other children after school hours. He seems guarded, angry, and hostile at times, withdrawn and sullen on other occasions. These problems at school have been worsening over the last few months and have led to the referral.

The evaluation of Bruce and his parents has gone relatively smoothly. It seems to you, after you have spent a few sessions with Bruce, that his problems in the school environment are the result of his reactions to children ridiculing and teasing him because of difficulty with his gait and with athletics. He has been hurt and has reacted with anger, defiance, and withdrawal.

You feel that work with Bruce in individual psychotherapy will be helpful to him in understanding his own reactions to the events at school, clarifying why other boys might pick on him, and discussing strategies for dealing with the ridicule he experiences. You also suspect that Bruce may have some longer standing concerns about his own body image, sense of self, and competence because of his birth injury and that an exploration of these issues may also be helpful. All these ideas, formulated in terms of a plan for psychotherapy with Bruce and his parents, are readily acceptable to them.

Your suggestion that a phone contact with Bruce's teacher to learn more about the school situation is accepted without hesitation by the parents, who have had ongoing discussions with the teacher and agree to tell her that you will be calling in the next week. Bruce, however, appears suddenly aghast, looking wounded as he hunches over slightly in his chair.

When Bruce heard you say that you would like to call Ms. Shiner and talk to her about the classroom and the problems Bruce may be having, he gasped meekly, "Why?"

You explain hurriedly: "I think it would be important to

ask if Ms. Shiner can help me learn more about the situation at
school. My talking with her may help us find ways that we can
work to make things better for you there." You had not expected Bruce to react so desperately to your suggestion of
involving his teacher.

"Leave her out of it," Bruce says angrily, recovering some
forcefulness.

"Bruce, would you tell me why you don't want me to
speak to Ms. Shiner?," you ask, only partly hiding your surprise at his response.

"She's a pain, too!," Bruce yells emphatically, striking the
angriest note you have yet heard from him.

"What do you mean?," you ask, noting that Bruce is
showing you the pattern Ms. Shiner has described to his
parents: initially shy and withdrawn, then increasingly angry
and defiant.

"She laughed the first day in school when I missed the ball
and fell," he says again becoming quiet, a tear in his eyes.

"Oh, I see," you respond empathically. "You think Ms.
Shiner makes fun of you too, like the kids do?"

Bruce says nothing, but his silence and his tears make it
clear that you have learned something important about why
school has become so difficult for him.

"Bruce," you say, "it's good that you've let me know how
you feel about Ms. Shiner. Tell me more about what happened
that first day."

After another moment or two, Bruce recounts the episode
in which, in his mind, Ms. Shiner laughed as he missed the ball
on the playground during lunch recess the first day of school.

You are impressed by his detailed memory. You listen and
allow Bruce to share his feelings about his teacher and his
impressions of how she has been uncaring toward him on
several occasions at school. Later in the session, you sense that
your empathy with Bruce's situation has allowed you to gain

more of his trust and to make him feel confident that you are his ally and will not take Ms. Shiner's and his classmates' side against him.

You are able to say: "Bruce, it's even more important than ever that I talk to Ms. Shiner now that you've told me what has happened in school and how she's been. I think that if she knows that we're working together and how you react to things that happen at school, she may be able to help you and I can talk with her to see if we can all work together to make things better."

Bruce still seems unconvinced, but not as resistant.

You decide that more reassurance about what you will discuss with Ms. Shiner is needed: "Bruce, when I talk to teachers or to anyone about a child whom I see in therapy, I always ask the parents and the child if it is alright first, and I only talk to the teacher if they say it is alright. I may talk to the teacher about problems that we are working on, but I try to not talk about details or parts that may be embarrassing or that the child may not want me to talk about. I also ask the child if there is anything that I should not say. That way, I can be careful to not say the wrong thing. Mainly, when I speak to a teacher the first time, I listen to what the teacher says. Is there anything you don't want me to say?," you ask Bruce, who seems reassured.

"Don't tell her I cry," he says poignantly.

"Alright, that's fine," you agree, realizing that Bruce's concern need not enter the discussion with the teacher and essential information can nonetheless be exchanged. You also make a mental note to talk to Bruce after you speak with Ms. Shiner and discuss the conversation with him in the context of his therapeutic needs.

This vignette illustrates, in relatively extreme form, the resistance a child may have to outside contacts made during the course of the therapy. Parents may have similar concerns, including anxiety over what others will reveal to the therapist, a sense of embarrassment or humiliation at others knowing their problems, or anxiety about losing the therapist as an ally.

It is generally very helpful to get first-hand accounts from teachers about problems children may be having in the school setting and, at times, to involve them in the treatment plan. Bruce's teacher in this vignette may or may not have acted as Bruce perceived. By speaking with her, you not only can gain a greater understanding of Bruce and his perception of events, but also may be able to influence how she interacts with Bruce and his schoolmates with regard to his disability.

If you meet resistance on the part of the child or parents to a contact with the teacher, you must explore the child's or family's thoughts about the discussion: what it will mean, what might be revealed, what will come of it, and other aspects. You should explain fully the intent of the discussion, what might come out of it, and how it may be helpful. You must explain confidentiality. As the foregoing vignette illustrates, you should also explore and understand what the child or family does not want discussed, so that the alliance with child and parents will be strengthened as the result of the school contact. The child and the parents should have a sense that the discussion with the teacher will be helpful to their own interests and will be another way in which you are showing your competence and concern by sensitively gathering information and working with whomever possible in order to help the child and family, while preserving their privacy and sense of special relationship with you.

When a Child Leaves the Session Early or Abruptly

Time spent in psychotherapy sessions is sometimes extremely difficult for children and adults. Reactions and feelings that are experienced by the patient may at times become nearly overwhelming. In order to escape from strongly experienced feelings or reactions toward themselves, others, or the therapist, children may express the desire to leave the session early, inquire hopefully about when the session will be over, or suddenly run out of the room.

The following vignette illustrates how a child's conflict over loyalties and reactions to parenting figures in his life caused him to flee from an intolerable conflict brought out in the therapy session and to try to escape to a safer place.

Max, age 10, has been in therapy with you for the past 6 months. He was referred because of school misbehavior, failing grades, poor peer relations, and two episodes in which he set fires in the garden of his home. During one session, while you and Max are talking about his mother's reluctance to let him spend a full weekend at his grandparents' home, he becomes visibly tense and angry, bolts from his chair without saying anything, and runs out of your office to the reception area, where his mother is waiting for him.

Bewildered by Max's sudden departure from the office, you quickly follow him. While walking to the reception area, you quickly review for yourself what may be occurring at this time in treatment.

Max had appeared more and more comfortable and open with you. He described feelings of loneliness at being an only child and especially upsetting reactions on coming home after school to an empty house. Both parents work outside the home, and at the age of 9, Max had been given a house key for use after school. He had to be given the key because several sitters and neighbors had been unable to supervise Max after school hours because of his noncompliant behavior. By the time he was referred to you, Max either stayed by himself or, on some occasions, went to a friend's house. In the last two months, Max had spontaneously begun walking to his grandparents' home after school. Their house is only half a mile from his own home.

Max's grandfather had retired a few months before from his carpentry work and was spending most of his time at home. He and Max had always enjoyed each other's company. The grandparents welcomed Max's visits, enjoyed helping him with his homework, and sometimes fed him dinner. Problems had arisen, however, because of the different parenting styles and expectations of Max's parents and grandparents. He has felt divided loyalties, confusion about expectations, and anger, especially at his mother, because of her expectations of stricter conformity to rules than was the case with her own parents.

When you arrive at the waiting room, you see Max seated in a red chair clinging to his startled mother's arm. Your clinical intuition suggests that perhaps the discussion in your office a few moments before had resulted in Max's feeling frightened or guilty at his own reactions that favored his grandparents over his mother and father and that he lost control and went to reunite with his mother. This, like so many difficult moments of high emotion, may be valuable clinically, but further discussion about Max's conflicts can wait. For now, he and his confused mother need to be reassured.

"Max," you say, "it seems that something we've been talking about in the session has made you upset. Let's go back to our room and see if we can understand what happened." You wait a moment, hoping that your presence alone will be supportive enough and that he will be able to give up his need for his mother's arm and return with you to the therapy room.

No luck. Max seems rooted to his chair, avoiding your eyes as he stares ahead. Another strategy might work. You try to see if you can speak with him alone for a few minutes about what happened. You would prefer to have him re-establish a sense of the ongoing work in therapy rather than go home with no sense of progress at this point, although the waiting room clock indicates that the time is nearly up and you have another session shortly.

Since Max bolted from your room because of personal feelings, you think it best to discuss his action confidentially. You explain to Max's mother that you would like to talk to Max alone for a few minutes here in the waiting area and ask her to step outside the room for a few minutes while you and he talk. Fortunately, she agrees.

That seems to do it. Max is by now able to let go of his mother's arm. You sit down by him and try to briefly go over what has happened. You begin by asking him what caused him to leave the room: "Max, what do you think upset you so much as we talked?"

"I don't know," he says quietly, fidgeting with some crayons on the table next to him.

"I don't know, either," you say honestly, although you have strong clinical suspicions that for now can be kept to yourself, given the intensity of Max's reaction. "Let's talk some more about it and see if we can understand what happened better."

Max remains in his chair.

You feel it necessary to remind Max of his rights in therapy: "Max, I suggested we talk more about what upset you, but you may not feel able to do that right now. That's alright. In our sessions, you can talk about problems as you wish; if you feel the time isn't right, we can do something else. I do not always know how you are feeling. Part of the therapy is your letting me know what you would like to talk about and what you do not want to talk about. That's something that I might not have explained well enough. Our time is nearly up for today, but let's go back into our therapy room for a few minutes."

Max, at your reassurance that he will not be trapped in a room and perhaps, in his estimation, forced to confess to his crimes, gets up and readily returns to the therapy room, where you spend a few minutes playing checkers, end the session, and arrange to see him next week.

You might have employed another strategy to continue the sense of therapeutic work and to define Max's need to leave the therapy room as a way of running from feelings within himself that were too difficult to "stay with" emotionally. By this strategy, you might have asked Max, while he was seated in the waiting room, if he would like his mother to join the two of you in the session. You would have to let Max himself make this decision, since he could easily interpret your suggestion that his mother join the session as a way of making him confront the conflict from which he had just run away.

Finally, if Max will not return to the therapy room regardless of your support, you would want to clarify generally for Max and his mother what has happened and to provide a framework for understanding the event as a part of the therapeutic process. You would also want to provide support if Max experiences further anxiety or difficulties when he gets home. To do this, you could tell Max and his mother that it seems as if Max has been upset by something that was discussed in the session. You hope that he will feel better once he is home and during the next few days. When you see him again next time, if he feels ready, you can discuss what upset him, but if he is not ready, then he does not have to talk about it. If he has any problems during the time until the next session, he or his mother should feel free to call you.

In this case, there was no suggestion that the child fleeing from the therapy room posed a physical danger to himself or others, and therefore the parent did not have to be involved at that time. The important point to emphasize when the child's abruptly leaving the therapy session poses no danger is that doing so often represents a way to escape feelings or reactions that are too difficult to bear. The question then becomes one of why these feelings are so difficult and how they can be understood in the therapy sessions. Support, reassurance, and clarification of the meaning of the sudden departure from the room may be helpful to children and parents who may feel guilty, angry, or embarrassed because of the child's apparent rejection of you.

Finally, there are numerous situations in which a particular child's sudden departure from your office can be understood as having a meaning other than flight from overwhelming emotion. Some common examples involve the child's immediate response to your statements or behavior. You may say or do something that makes the child angry, such as winning a game and not realizing that the child is losing his or her self-esteem in the process, or asking the child to help clean up the room after playing or drawing, a task that the child may simply reject and leave to you to do.

The child may also want to test you by seeing what your reaction to an early departure will be. In another case, a child may become overwhelmed by the feeling that he or she is becoming too personally attached to and dependent on you and leave the room, afraid of these feelings. In other examples, a child will leave, expressing a need such as going to the bathroom, getting a drink, feeling ill, or wanting to show a parent something he or she has just made, perhaps a clay sculpture.

Occasional early or abrupt departures may be expected and do not necessarily need comment or extensive exploration. When they seem to occur at crucial moments or become frequent or repetitive, however, greater understanding of their meaning is necessary.

DIFFICULT MOMENTS INVOLVING MATERIAL OBJECTS IN PSYCHOTHERAPY

When a Child Wants You to Buy Something

It is both expected and desirable for the child in psychotherapy to have thoughts and feelings about the therapist during the times between psychotherapy sessions. The child's reactions to the therapist often result in an attempt to integrate the therapist into other areas of the child's life. Sometimes this attempted integration results in the therapist being treated in a manner that appears similar to the way the child would treat a neighbor or a friend. This blurring of boundaries may occur in a host of situations, one being that the child asks the therapist to be a customer or buyer of goods. Such situations may be both amusing and important for the therapy. The following vignette is typical.

Barbara is a 10-year-old girl who has been doing well in therapy. Her crying spells, whining, and enuresis have all stopped. In your psychotherapy sessions with her you and she have been learning more about the anxiety that seems to have been the basis for her regression from a previously normal level of functioning.

One day, Barbara comes to the session with a large brown bag under her arm. At the outset of the session, she pulls a box of Girl Scout cookies out of her bag and asks if you would like to buy a box. Since the bag seems large enough for three or four boxes, you get the feeling that if you say yes, you could become the week's biggest customer.

There are several ways of handling the situation. One
You wonder why you have been selected as a potential
buyer. Asking you to buy what she is selling may be Barbara's way of asking you to accept her or something she offers—as a way of saying you find her acceptable or valuable,
a feeling she may doubt you have on its own merits. Barbara
may also be asking you to prove what she may want to believe but doubts—that she is "special" to you, more "special" than other children you see, and that you will therefore
save her the bother of knocking on neighborhood doors to
sell the cookies. Having you "cornered" and in a position in
which it is socially difficult to say "No" establishes a certain
power and control over you and the situation and may be her
way of trying to command your allegiance and feelings for
her.

On the other hand, Barbara may also be trying to prove
her competence and yours by showing you her more "grown-
up" side in selling or acting to make money—quite an advance
for a previously whining, enuretic girl. Any of these or other
reasons for her actions may seem compelling to you.

Alternatively, you may decide to think in a more concrete and straightforward manner—not necessarily a bad
strategy at all—and conclude that you are one of the few
grown-ups Barbara knows and she very likely assumes that
you, like other grown-ups, have more money to buy cookies
than her 10-year-old friends have. Barbara may quite inno-
cently think nothing of trying to tap into your financial re-
sources to sell her quota of Girl Scout cookies.

In any case, you have several hypotheses, but very likely
feel that you must do something now, since the box of
cookies is already on the table between you and your patient.
Barbara seems eager to exchange it for a few dollars of your
lunch money.

way to begin is to try and explore with Barbara some of the symbolic possibilities for what she may be saying through her salesperson role about your relationship with her. Leave the cookies on the table—both actually and metaphorically—and begin making general introductory and facilitating comments about the situation and what may be going on, for example, "I hadn't realized it was already the time of year when Girl Scout cookies are sold." See what she has to say. Perhaps she will elaborate and give you more information. After awhile, you can try to get to the heart of the matter with comments like, "I wonder what it was that made you feel I'd be a person you'd like to sell cookies to?" A discussion along these lines, if Barbara is able to talk about motivation and her relationship with you in this manner, may allow to happen what you would like to happen: Barbara's reflecting on the meaning of her desire to sell you the cookies, followed by her understanding that the two of you should be exploring the meanings of feelings and behavior in your sessions, but not acting on the basis of these feelings.

All this insight may sound good, but is quite a bit to expect from many children, especially preadolescents. You may be able, though, to combine such an approach with one of the following options.

Go ahead and buy a box of the cookies. Pick the type you like best. Give her the money and thank her. Tell Barbara that one box is enough; you do not need all three.

By acting in this way, you have surrendered your lunch money, but you can always eat the cookies for lunch. You have acted socially in an appropriate manner, gotten some good cookies, and put some limits on Barbara's grandiose fantasies that you would satisfy all her needs, since you did not buy all three boxes. You have also shown Barbara that you do care for her and will try to please her. You may also be setting yourself up to buy a raffle ticket for the fifth-grade class outing next month, but maybe then you will win a TV set.

Alternatively, on a more serious note, your exploration of the symbolic meaning of the sale, along with your actually buying the cookies, may make Barbara feel both cared for and supported. She will also realize that such events have meaning in the therapy. They will be noted, and discussed and become a part of the therapeutic work. She may, however, not feel rejected or angry in the present, especially if you think the therapeutic alliance is still tenuous and will not be helped by your refusal to buy her cookies right now.

The other option is to not buy the cookies. You can tell Barbara that the cookies look very good and you hope she will be able to sell them all. You think it best, however, that you not buy any. That is because you and she have a unique relationship in which her feelings and reactions and problems are discussed in a special way. This relationship is different from other relationships. The two of you have been making progress in understanding her better. You are concerned that by buying and selling things in a manner that is similar to what people do in stores or in the neighborhood, the two of you would take something from your work together and deprive it of its special character.

The next thing to do is to ask Barbara how she feels about what you have said. She may or may not offer a reaction at that point. If at that time or later on you sense particular reactions in Barbara, such as feelings of rejection, or even of gratitude and relief, you may be able to use these reactions therapeutically or comment on them and relate them to what has happened and to your relationship.

A final question: What if you really like Girl Scout cookies and think Barbara is offering you a real bargain? Answer: Act as if you are neutral about Girl Scout cookies and would really prefer to save your money for lunch, as in the example. Follow one of the approaches suggested above. Sacrifice your sweet tooth for the sake of a therapeutic approach that involves very limited if any actual purchases from your patients. Avoid the associated, possibly confusing meanings for the child.

When a Child Brings Gifts to You

Unlike Barbara, the 10-year-old girl in the previous example who brought Girl Scout cookies to sell, Sarah, the 8-year-old girl in this example, brings you a box of cookies as a gift.

Giving gifts and selling goods both result in the therapist's acquiring material objects, but may be different in other ways. Unlike the selling of goods, the giving of gifts may convey a deeper sense of attachment and emotion, since reciprocity or return on a concrete level is not necessarily required. The meaning of the action, be it giving gifts or selling articles, nonetheless often reflects specific issues in the therapy at the time.

Presents can provide a way for your patients to give you something of themselves, to ask you to accept something about themselves, or to manipulate you to give something back in return. Gifts may also serve as vehicles to thank you for having already accepted something about or done something for the giver.

Sarah's presenting problems included poor school performance, nightmares, and angry outbursts. These problems are improved now, although she did exhibit the latest in a series of angry outbursts and crying spells during your last session. Her arrival with a box of cookies for today's session was unexpected. Is Sarah thanking you for accepting a part of her that she thought was unacceptable? Is she expressing her gratitude to you for helping her with her problems? Presents may also be attempts to ask the therapist to like the child more. How is Sarah's self-esteem? Learning about herself and sharing feelings with you in the sessions may have been difficult for her. She may want you to love and accept her and may be trying to buy those feelings. On the other hand, she may feel that she already has your approval and wants to thank you for it or to assure herself of its continuation.

In a somewhat different light, Sarah may be anxious about her angry outburst last week and be bringing the cookies as a peace offering, a way of saying, "I'm sorry I did that," or, "Please like me even though I did that."

The choice of the cookies instead of some other present may also be symbolically important. Whether Sarah thought of the idea herself or was encouraged to bring the cookies by her parents is also important, and you want to remember to explore this with the parents if the opportunity arises after you are sure they know about the present. This can be ascertained by asking Sarah whether they are aware of her intended present to you.

As is often the case, the therapy and your child patient can benefit from a caring and warm exploration of the symbolical and interpersonal meaning of the gift. You might start by thanking Sarah for bringing you a gift and asking her how she decided to give it to you: "How did you decide that you wanted to give *me* a gift?"

The exploration of meaning with the child also can be helpful in deciding whether you will actually accept the gift. Ideally, the gift should be understood and dealt with on the basis of its psychological meaning. If this is done completely and well, the tangible gift is not necessary and may be "not accepted" without arousing feelings of rejection or anger or other negative feelings in the patient. Gifts should not be encouraged. The world in which you work is often largely a symbolic one. The world outside your office is partly symbolic, too, but meanings and relationships are expressed more by action and in more physical, concrete terms there.

This said, some tempering statements of our lofty idealism about gifts in therapy are in order. While gifts should not be encouraged, some therapists accept small gifts from patients occasionally and do not emphasize exploration of the situation psychologically unless the practice becomes repetitive, or the presents have obvious personal meaning in the context of the sessions, or the presents are large and extravagant. For many child (and adult) patients, tangible and concrete expressions of feelings may be necessary at times. A totally symbolic realm may not be sufficient or satisfying. Accepting the child by accepting the present may at times be helpful to both the child and the therapy.

Some therapists allow the gift and the expression of whatever the gift means psychologically, but limit the practice to certain times, for example, at Christmas or Hanukkah season. Such times of the year are socially approved giftgiving times, and gifts to therapists at those times may reflect social convention to some degree. This can make it easier to give the gift and thereby facilitate more personal underlying expressions to emerge and be discussed. If this is the option you prefer in your practice, you would explore the meaning of the gift with Sarah, but also say that you have made a rule in your office that you do not accept gifts from your patients except at Christmas or Hanukkah time, when some kids and their parents like to give gifts and some do not. Either way is alright with you.

Another approach to the situation, if the gift is not too extravagant, is to explore its meaning in terms of the relationship, then accept it. Emphasize, though, that the special relationship you and the child have means that you try to understand the feelings that result in people's giving gifts. As a rule, gifts are not accepted or used in your work together. In this way, the child need not feel rejected for having already brought the gift, and you have treated him or her in a personal, "special" way, thus perhaps satisfying the child's need to be "special." You have also, however, set up a standard for the work you are doing. If the child later breaks this standard, the infraction can be explored not only in terms of the gift's meaning, but also in terms of why the child thought it necessary to bring a gift, given that the rule about not giving you gifts had been made clear.

A final word about gifts: Some therapists give small gifts to their patients at times, although others are against the practice and feel that giving gifts to patients conveys messages of a psychological nature that should be left to be understood in the context of the work and not acted upon. For us, the most acceptable context for gifts to be given by therapists, if given at all, would be at the termination of therapy, when both child and therapist may want to give the other some small remembrance of the work done together.

Sometimes a personally written note or card to the child at that time (or at Christmas or Hanukkah time) can be a meaningful present. If you feel that a gift to the child would be helpful, a card with a personal message about the work done together, wishes for the future, and other sentiments has the advantage of both being something tangible and expressing the essence of the shared work in a direct and individual manner. The child can also keep the card to reread as a reminder.

When a Child Asks to Take Play Materials from Your Office

As the previous example illustrates, gift-giving between child and therapist may have many meanings, on both concrete and symbolic levels. The child who asks for or expects to be given office play materials provides a variation on this theme.

Darryl is a small, likeable 7-year-old boy who has been in treatment with you for 10 weeks. His history includes physical abuse, a chronically unstable home environment, several foster home placements, and presenting problems of shyness, tearful withdrawal from social interactions, and "daydreaming" in school.

Psychotherapeutic work with Darryl has gone well. He reportedly looks forward to the weekly sessions, he has begun to talk about events in school and the current home environment, and his occasional smiles break through a previously somber, withdrawn affect.

For the last few sessions, Darryl has been playing with a series of miniature cars and trucks in the office. He has been careful to divide the vehicles equally between the two of you and has structured the traffic in the automobile games so as to avoid collisions between your cars or trucks and his. He seems to favor a small green truck that has headlights that move from side to side, doors and a trunk that open and shut, and "Fix-It Company" in large black lettering on the side.

Toward the end of the current session, while putting the trucks and cars back in their box, Darryl delays putting the green one back, closes the almost full cardboard box, and puts the box on the shelf. Soon he begins to move toward the door and says "Bye," still clutching the green truck.

You try to be helpful: "Darryl, you forgot to put away the green truck."

"Oh, yeah," Darryl replies, as he puts the truck down on the shelf and hastily exits.

You sigh to yourself in relief. Darryl has complied and you have avoided a confrontation. His desire for the small truck seems to signify his deprivation. You wish you could give him this and other presents as well.

The next week, you are not as lucky. Darryl has been playing with a sleek-looking yellow car. At clean-up time, he

again helps you put the other cars and trucks away, but then, while holding the yellow car, says with an imploring look, "Can I take this one home?"

It is important to think symbolically here, as always in psychotherapy sessions, and to consider possible meanings the car has to Darryl. It is also important to think about what your allowing him to take something from the office will mean to him and to you about the relationship.

Yet Darryl has made his important request, as many requests, statements, and questions in therapy are made, at the end of a session, with no time to discuss the material at length. You could say to him that you would like to talk about his wanting the car next time and discuss it then. For now, though, he should leave the car in the office.

This approach leaves things ambiguous and allows you a temporary reprieve from feeling guilty about rejecting Darryl and his request, but it also leaves open the chance of his actually getting the car, a possibility that should not be encouraged.

Perhaps a better approach to take at this time, although a more difficult one, is to say, kindly and directly, that play material in the office is for the use of all the children you treat. You cannot allow some children to take things home or keep toys, because if you did, the toys would not be available for other children and some toys Darryl wants would not be available for him. You can then add that you and he can talk more about this next time. You can also mention that you do allow children to take pictures, drawings, or tracings of things they have made in your office home with them if they wish, or to leave them with you in individual boxes or folders labeled with their names that you keep in your office. In this way, Darryl can be told that if he wants to think about or remember your sessions between times, he can have drawings at home to look at.

All this, of course, will nonetheless be a disappointment for Darryl, who wants the car and, as much or more, wants you and your special caring for him through the gift of the car. A drawing is a partial substitute that probably will not seem nearly as good for awhile.

During the course of the week, you remember Darryl's reluctant compliance and his putting the yellow car down as he hurriedly left the session. You remember his downcast eyes avoiding yours. Although you feel badly for depriving Darryl of what he has wanted so badly, you now have more time to think about his request and its meaning. You think about further strategies to use in trying to make the difficult moment have a beneficial effect in your work with him.

Darryl has shown you that he has a particular attraction to cars and trucks. This attraction may have several meanings. Boys his age are often attracted to toy vehicles. For some children, they seem to represent the possibilities of independence, assertiveness, and mobility and the chance to identify with older people who are more free and appear to be in more control of their own lives and destinies. Cars, trucks, or other vehicles may, however, have additional, particular meanings to Darryl based on his own background. Information of this nature may be helpful and can also serve as an entry point for the further discussion about his request for the car that you should consider for the next session. If he does not bring up the topic, you may want to introduce it.

You should also realize, however, that it is not just the car, but your giving the car to him—and perhaps, too, your giving him something other children also want from you— that is so important to Darryl. If you were to give him the toy, you would possibly be saying that you are willing to give a part of yourself to him. You may be implying to him that he is special to you, perhaps more special than others, and that he is worthy of your presents, which he probably doubts, given his history. He may be led to believe that in some sense, you will give him the nurturance that he has thus far lacked or, on a more concrete level, that you will give him the toys and play articles he does not have enough of at home.

Assuming Darryl does not bring up the topic of the car in the next session, you might start by noting what he has chosen to play with this time. If he chooses or does not choose the car again, you might comment on how his play material compares with last week's choice.

At some point, you might say that you had been thinking about the car he liked so much and were wondering how he felt about your not giving it to him last week. He may or may not be able to say something in response. If he is not able to discuss it, you might reflect on the situation for him. You could tell him that you realize that you and he have developed an important and close relationship over the last few months while working together to understand the problems he has had, and that it is natural for people who are close to want to exchange presents or sometimes share belongings with one another. The toys in the office are for all the children who come to therapy, however, and cannot be taken out of the office. That does not mean that the relationship you have is not special; it is a special relationship that is important to both of you. The rules may sometimes be hard to understand, but you feel that following them will help you and him to work well together.

You might also say that you realize that things you do or say, or things about the way you are, may at times make Darryl have different kinds of feelings. Anger, for example, may be one of these feelings. You would like to talk to him about those feelings when he has them. You think it will help him in dealing with his problems and in your work together.

2

Difficult Moments Reconsidered

This chapter discusses another possible approach to understanding how difficult moments arise in psychotherapy with children. Herein, we suggest that the child's, parents', and therapist's implicit expectations concerning the process and meaning of therapy may be in conflict and thus give rise to difficult moments of several types. This view is explained in the text and illustrated with examples.

The preface provided several general guidelines that the authors felt would be helpful to therapists in dealing with difficult moments that occur in psychotherapy with children. Chapter 1 presented a series of vignettes intended to exemplify difficult moments that might occur in working with children and ways to both understand and manage these problematic events. In this chapter, we wish to discuss other perspectives on difficult moments in child psychotherapy—events that facilitate or retard therapeutic progress.

There is a large body of literature on psychotherapy with children. We present the issues relevant to difficult moments within the context of commonly accepted tenets of psychotherapeutic events. We wish to point out that difficult moments invariably occur in almost every process of psychotherapy with children, yet there has been no specific focus on these events in the literature. We present the view that these difficult moments occur in psychotherapy with children because children, parents, and psychotherapists often have numerous beliefs, assumptions, and expectations concerning the nature, course, and conduct of psychotherapy. When these expectations or assumptions are understood differently by the child, parents, or therapist, or when they are presented on an apparently practical or concrete level by the therapist, but are challenged by the child or parents on a more interpersonal or symbolic level, difficult moments occur in the psychotherapy. We are not saying that difficult moments in psychotherapy cannot occur for other reasons, but we wish to suggest that an understanding of problematic reactions on the part of child patients to what appear to be straightforward expectations regarding the therapy often result from conflicts in these expectations. Understanding these conflicts can clarify how and why many of these difficult moments occur.

Several of these conflicting expectations concerning the phases, relationships, and activities of psychotherapy with children are discussed in the following pages, with examples of how challenges to apparently straightforward expectations may produce difficult moments. It is our hope that this discussion will aid you in understanding such difficult moments.

The difficult moments themselves are illustrated more fully in the vignettes presented in Chapter 1. We wish to emphasize that the behaviors described in the vignettes may represent examples of challenges to more than one expectation. Thus, a difficult moment may have many meanings and is best understood within the context of the situation from which it arises.

EXPECTATION: The child has a psychological problem or conflict that results in unwanted feelings or behaviors.

Psychotherapists of several theoretical orientations would hold that children with deviant behaviors or maladaptive or troubling feelings are not "bad" but rather manifest feelings, attitudes, or behavioral patterns that result from inherited personality tendencies or interpersonal and/or situational experiences that have caused the undesirable emotions, reactions, or behaviors (A. Freud, 1966; Whitten, Pettit, and Fischoff, 1969; Pruett and Dahl, 1982; Rutter, 1982; McDermott and Char, 1984; Pfeffer, 1984, 1986; Swanson and Biaggio, 1985; Lamb, 1986). Psychotherapists' beliefs often emphasize that children's behaviors are determined by the interactions of conscious, unconscious, and experiential factors (Powell, 1973; Patterson, 1974; Taylor, 1976; Yarrow and Harmon, 1980; Rutter, 1981a,b; Group for the Advancement of Psychiatry—Committee on Child Psychiatry, 1982; Rutter and Giller, 1982).

Parents and children, however, do not always agree with these basic assumptions of therapists. Many children and parents do not accept the view that the child has feelings or reactions that are unknown to the child or are related to previous or current experiences that are affecting the child's behavior or mood. Furthermore, many children and parents often oversimplify or have rigid views of behavior. They believe that behavior defined by parents and teachers as "good" is the only acceptable behavior. Furthermore, there is often a belief that children who have other behaviors are "bad", whether or not the children are aware of the motivations for their behaviors or are able to behave otherwise.

The discrepancies in the views of therapist, child, and parents with respect to the nature of the child's behavior can have important effects on the progress of psychotherapy and may contribute to numerous difficult moments in the therapy. These difficult moments may include: (a) resistance by the child to coming to therapy at all in the face of any inkling that a new set of assumptions about behavior is possible; (b) abrupt termination of therapy when acceptance or understanding of the concept that problems occur because of internal reactions becomes too difficult or threatens parent–child, parent, or family equilibrium; or (c) running from the therapy room to escape a new, confusing, and frightening viewpoint of oneself or the family, rather than staying in a place where internal feelings and attitudes of both positive and negative nature are allowed and encouraged.

EXPECTATION: Individual psychotherapy can be effective in reducing the child's internal problem, conflict, unwanted feelings, or behavior.

Although there is some empirical research supporting the expectation of therapists that child psychotherapy will have a beneficial outcome, results of research on the effects of psychotherapy are variable and controversial (Heinicke and Strassman, 1975; Wright, Moelis, and Pollack, 1976; Kazdin and Wilson, 1978; Howlin, Marchant, Rutter, Berger, Hersov, and Yule, 1984; Rutter, 1982; Shaffer, 1984; Casey and Berman, 1985; T. Shapiro and Esman, 1985; Weisz, 1986). Nevertheless, the basic tenet of anyone committed to doing psychotherapy with children is that through psychotherapy, the child can be helped to be happier, better functioning, and more content (Haworth, 1964; Gardner, 1971; Carek, 1972; Adams, 1974; Tseng and McDermott, 1975; McDermott and Harrison, 1977; Winnicott, 1971; Group for the Advancement of Psychiatry—Committee on Child Psychiatry, 1982). In fact, psychotherapy with children may be defined as any face-to-face psychological intervention regardless of its theoretical base (Shaffer, 1984). Its goals are considered to be reduction of target symptoms or problems, enhancement of social adjustment, promotion of normal development with enhancement of autonomy and self-reliance, generalization of improvement in the child's behavior from the treatment setting to other situations, ensuring continuation of improvement,

and a focus on changing the environment to make it supportive of the child's growth and development (Rutter, 1982;
Shaffer, 1984).

When the therapeutic process does not seem to work
quickly enough, parents often raise questions about the effec-
tiveness of the therapy. Sometimes, as noted above, the child
or the parents are so resistant to letting go of their beliefs
about the child's behavioral or emotional problems that they
cannot appreciate that a new way of looking at the problem
may be effective. Such resistance on the part of the parents
and/or the child may arise because of personal fears, internal
conflicts, and defenses. The parents' particular attitudes toward child–rearing, their own childhood experiences, and/or
their acceptance of certain of society's negative views about
psychological problems may also constitute impediments to
appreciating the benefits of psychotherapy for their child.
Parents with these attitudes may not give the therapeutic
process very much of a chance to work, or they may not
ascribe to the therapy the positive changes that have occurred
in the child.

Lack of trust, expressions of anger, disillusionment, or
frustration of the parents and/or the child often result in difficult moments in the therapy. These conflicts may manifest
themselves in missed sessions, late arrivals, abrupt termination, or the child's showing aggression toward the therapist,
destroying the therapist's property, or refusing to speak during psychotherapy sessions.

EXPECTATION: Psychotherapy involves a unique relationship with a professionally trained psychotherapist.

The patient–therapist relationship is a crucial factor in
effective psychotherapy with children (Levinson and Kitchener, 1966; Hicks, 1974; Kolvin, Garside, Nicol, MacMillan,

Wolstenholme, and Leitch, 1981; Shaffer, 1984). Traux and Carlshuff (1967) suggested that in work with adult patients, the best psychotherapeutic outcomes were apparant when therapists were sensitive to the patient's feelings, were able to communicate their understanding in clear language, and provided an atmosphere of trust, warmth, and acceptance. In a similar vein, it would seem that these observations also apply to child psychotherapy. The therapist believes that through a caring, supportive, carefully monitored relationship, the child's reactions and conflicts may be observed, understood, and modified in such a way that the child's development can progress and conflicts will be resolved (Strupp, 1975; Frank, 1976). The therapist tries to facilitate a therapeutic alliance or a contract with the child by establishing an atmosphere of high motivation to work collaboratively in treatment (McConville, 1976). The basic assumption of a therapeutic alliance or a treatment contract is that regardless of the vicissitudes of feelings, reactions, behaviors, or life events, the child and therapist will work together in treatment with an explicit goal of helping the child with symptom and conflict reduction (Shaffer, 1984; T. Shapiro and Esman, 1985).

The child may have little cognitive understanding of what a "therapeutic alliance" is. The child may, however, view the therapist in many ways. The therapist may be seen, for example, as an adult who is loving, omnipotent, and kind, on one hand, or hostile, impotent, and despicable, on the other. Indeed, the therapist may be, from the child's point of view, a person with any of a number of characteristics. The child may have no sense of what "help" means and no sense of having a "problem." The child's assumptions about the "special" relationship with the therapist may express itself by desires for special care or love that have not been experienced in the relationship with the parents.

The therapist understands that many of the child's reactions involve transference responses. Such transference responses involve feelings, attitudes, and behaviors toward the therapist that are derived from unconscious reactions of the child toward other emotionally meaningful people (S. Freud, 1962; Brody, 1961; A. Freud, 1965; Marshall, 1979; Cantor and Kestenbaum, 1986). The therapist who understands the derivation of the child's transference reactions can discuss the genesis of these reactions with the child and help the child to develop insight about reactions to other people (Olden, 1953; Fraiberg, 1962; Anthony, 1964; A. Freud, 1965; Markowitz, 1964; Gardner, 1971, 1975; Winnicott, 1971; Klein, 1973; Stirtzinger, 1983; McDermott and Char, 1984). The main task for the therapist is to help the child understand transference responses and at the same time maintain a therapeutic alliance.

The child's assumptions about having a special person to relate to on a regular basis may lead the child to test the limits of the psychotherapeutic relationship to see if it can provide the kind of love, caring, support, and help that may be desired from but inadequately provided by parents or other important adults. These assumptions and wishes of the child, which are often based on transference reactions, challenge the therapeutic alliance and set the stage for numerous difficult moments that become part of the psychotherapeutic process. In typical difficult moments, the child: does not want to leave the session because of a need for more contact, feels entitled to more time than allotted in the session, or insists that he or she be allowed to take a puppet or toy home from the playroom.

EXPECTATION: At intervals during the psychotherapy, the parents will usually have sessions with the therapist. Unless a new contract is stated, the main focus of these sessions will be on understanding how the child's attitudes, feelings, and behaviors occur in the context of the child's life experience.

For the most part, psychotherapists treating children arrange meetings with the parents to exchange information about the child and to provide guidance to the parents (Bernal, Klinnert, and Schultz, 1980; Group for the Advancement of Psychiatry—Committee on Child Psychiatry, 1982; Griest, Forehand, Rogers, Breiner, Furey, and Williams, 1982; Rutter, 1982; Dulcan, 1984; Shaffer, 1984). This approach aims to promote parental insight about the child's feelings and behaviors and to offer the parents an opportunity to discuss concrete and specific ways of interacting with their child.

Parents may initially assume that the focus of their discussions with the therapist will be on the reactions and attitudes of their child that are problematic to them. They may come to realize, however, that children's problems very commonly reflect the strengths and weaknesses of the parenting they have received (Gluck, Tanner, Sullivan, Erickson, and Gluck, 1964; D'Angelo and Walsh, 1967; Howlin, Marchant, Rutter, Berger, Hersov, and Yule, 1973; Reisinger, Frangia, and Hoffman, 1976; Small and Teagno, 1980, Strain, Glass, and Miller, 1980; Ricks, 1982; Rutter, 1982). Indeed, parents often either come to or resist and defend against the realization that their own conflicts and psychological problems have contributed to their child's problematic feelings or behaviors. If the parents are unable to accept and deal adaptively with this realization, their inability may be communicated to the child in either conscious or unconscious ways. The child's behavior in psychotherapy sessions may therefore be related to parental anxieties that create numerous difficult moments. Angry outbursts resulting in destruction of toys or throwing of objects may reflect the child's responses to changes in family interactions that are prompted by parental resistance to the realization of their own internal problems. A child's refusing to come to the session from the waiting area or hitting the therapist in the session may reflect the parents' anger. The child's announcement of a wish to stop treatment may create a difficult moment that reflects, not the child's decision, but the parents' resistance to the insights gained in their "parent guidance" sessions with the therapist.

Parents may also find the child's relationship with the therapist confusing, frightening, or competitive. While a special relationship between child and therapist may have appeared helpful initially, some parents may come to regard it as a threat to their influence, position, or control vis-á-vis the child. Abrupt termination, late arrivals at sessions, and missed appointments may all be difficult moments that result from parental conflicts engendered by the therapist's unique relationship with their child.

EXPECTATION: The child–therapist relationship will continue until the child's problems, conflicts, unwanted feelings, or behaviors are relieved.

In the beginning phase of treatment with the child, clear goals are established. For example, one therapeutic goal may be to help a child who refuses to attend school resume daily attendance. Another may be to decrease a child's despair and suicidal ideation (Pfeffer, 1986). Termination of treatment can be considered when the goals have been achieved (Cantor and Kestenbaum, 1986). Termination must be planned collaboratively by the child, parents, and therapist.

The child may believe or wish that this important and nurturing relationship will last forever. By not accepting the reality of separation, the child can deny the fear of loss. Some children fear loss of the relationship with the therapist so much that they stop progressing in their therapy. In this way, they avoid having to experience the loss that will come if therapy is "successful" and their problems are resolved. In the termination phase of therapy, some children create difficult moments by regression, severe anger displays, refusal to leave the therapy room, or refusal to come to therapy.

Difficult moments also arise from special circumstances that challenge the child's and parents' expectations that therapy will last until the child's symptoms are resolved. There are numerous circumstances that result in premature termination of therapy (Levitt, 1957, 1963; Ross and Lacey, 1961; McAdoo and Roeske, 1973; Horenstein and Hauston, 1976; Novick, Benson, and Rembar, 1981; Beitchman and Dielman, 1983). Typical such circumstances are that the child's family moves, the psychotherapy trainee's time at the training center comes to an end, or the therapist moves or takes another job. The child's anger at the therapist may be a response to perceived abandonment. Loss or feelings of rejection can create numerous difficult moments that may take many forms. For example, the child may steal articles from the playroom, demand to take home objects that were made during therapy, try to destroy materials or break toys, or miss sessions with the therapist. Difficult moments of this type are often painful for the therapist, who may feel guilty for leaving the child before treatment has been successfully completed.

EXPECTATION: The psychotherapy sessions are a special time during which the child can play, behave, or talk in whatever way he or she wishes; only violence toward self or others and destruction of property are not allowed.

The therapist tries to promote a treatment atmosphere of openness and trust. Furthermore, because children's cognitive skills, communication capacities, impulse control, and affect expression are not mature, children cannot be expected to relate to a therapist entirely on a verbal level. In fact, playing is a natural form of expression for children. Therefore, most formats of child psychotherapy include telling stories and play with toys and drawings as means of facilitating communication and the therapeutic process (Olden, 1953; Fraiberg, 1962; Anthony, 1964; A. Freud, 1964; Markowitz, 1964; Gardner, 1971, 1972; Winnicott, 1971; Klein, 1973; Ornstein, 1976, 1981; Stirtzinger, 1983; McDermott and Char, 1984; Alger, Linn, and Beardslee, 1985; Oster and Gould, 1987).

Many children are excited by the opportunity to spend time with a caring, interested, attentive adult doing nearly anything they want to do. Other children find such an open-ended, unstructured opportunity to talk and play frightening for a number of reasons that then create difficult moments in the therapy. For example, some children are afraid to be separated from their parents or to go anywhere with a strange adult. Some children realize quite rightly that engagement in activities with another person is actually the beginning of an involvement and a relationship with that person. This potential relationship may be confusing and anxiety-provoking, especially since it is centered around the child's "problems" or "feelings." Some children are distrustful of all adults except their parents and become confused and frightened at being alone in a room with an adult regardless of how many toys and play articles are available. Some children fear that the toys and play articles are just a pretense and that the real purpose in being with the therapist is to extract confessions of wrongdoing or to receive punishment or a lecture similar to those they may have already been subjected to by parents or teachers. Some children are uncertain and anxious about what the therapist may expect or require of them in the session.

A difficult moment when a child has one of these reactions may come when the child refuses to come with the therapist, is unable or refuses to separate from the parent, refuses to relate, play, or talk in the playroom, or flees from the room. Some children create difficult moments because they do not believe it possible for them to have the attention and caring of an adult who will allow them freedom to talk and play in any way they wish. Such children may throw or destroy articles, perhaps indicating that they do not feel they merit the freedom they have been given. These children must challenge what has happened or create a situation in which they expect to be punished, such as by climbing recklessly on tables, throwing articles, or painting on the walls.

EXPECTATION: The psychotherapy sessions will occur at a set time and at regular intervals that have been arranged in advance, usually once or twice a week.

The need to establish a definite schedule for the psychotherapy sessions is an expectation that few parents or children challenge when the contract for the therapy is discussed. A schedule that sets the length of therapy sessions, the time interval between sessions, and the times of meeting establishes a sense of continuity and orientation for the child, the therapist, and the parents. Deviations from this time frame can be evaluated as to their meanings with regard to the child's conflicts or symptoms.

Establishing a schedule for the sessions creates a special circumstance that has its own rules, movement, and agenda. It promotes effective psychotherapy (Heinicke, 1965, 1969; Barrett, Hampe, and Miller, 1978; Looney, 1984; Shaffer, 1984; Heinicke and Ramsey-Klee, 1968). A definite time for and regularity of the sessions suggest that the child is able to release himself or herself from everyday rhythms and routines and step into a time lock from which he or she, with the therapist, can look into other aspects of the child's life. This engagement in therapeutic work often carries with it anxiety and ambivalence. Conforming to this regular psychotherapy time is often very difficult for children and families, and the previously agreed-upon expectation that having regular hours will facilitate the psychotherapy is soon challenged by the child and/or the parents.

One challenge to this assumption is the anxiety of the child, who, in the face of regularly scheduled sessions, is forced to acknowledge that there are ongoing problems and anxieties that cannot be avoided but must be dealt with regularly and consistently. Regularly scheduled sessions may also imply to the child and/or the parents that the therapist may not always be available, suggesting that there are restraints on the possible expectations or hopes parents or children have for an omnipotent figure who will always be there for them. Children frequently have difficulty accepting that a relationship as important as that with the therapist will be available to them only a few hours a week.

Another facet of therapy is that a time limit for the therapy session is established. The patient must therefore express issues of immediate and symbolic importance within a time context. A time limit for the therapy session serves as a catalyst to focus on relevant issues. The assumption that sessions with the therapist will have a time limit and that the therapist will have appointments with other children is frequently challenged. Functioning well within the time constraints of a psychotherapy session requires both a degree of control that the child may not have and the ability to accept the limits imposed by the needs of another important person—the therapist.

Many children become very attached to their therapists and relive, in their therapy, the anxiety about separation from parenting figures that they have experienced earlier in their lives. Some children get so involved in the themes of their play, which reflect the crucial psychological themes of their internal needs and conflicts, that they have great difficulty stopping an activity and resuming everyday concerns. Other children become so anxious when they express crucial themes in their play that they must leave or flee before the session is scheduled to end. These reactions of children to the expectations and limits of the therapeutic hour create many difficult moments such as coming late to the session, wanting to leave the session early, dawdling in the cleanup phase of the session, and refusing to leave the session at the end of the hour.

EXPECTATION: The psychotherapy sessions will always oc-
                cur in the same place, usually the therapist's
                office or a designated play area.

It is assumed that a single designated room or play area will facilitate the psychotherapy by providing security, continuity, and knowledge of where the furniture, toys, and games are located. A fixed location for therapy sessions allows the child to continue discussing themes or to use familiar play objects that were left at the last session. It fosters the elaboration of complex themes and makes it possible to repeat play and/or behaviors as a way of working out conflicts. Such working through conflictual issues is an essential aspect of psychotherapy (McDermott and Char, 1984). It enables a child to practice new behaviors, reconsider problematic fantasies, and strengthen newly acquired adaptive skills. The designated room or play area becomes a special place in which there is created an environment that facilitates learning about the child's reaction and conflicts.

On a more symbolic level, however, acceptance of this

special place may imply an acceptance of the unique therapeutic work and expression that are allowed and fostered in that place. Not all children can accept or engage in the therapeutic relationship or the therapeutic work. Some children express this problem and create difficult moments by refusing to enter the room at the beginning of the session, constantly leaving the room to go to the bathroom, requesting that the therapist take them outside to play or get a drink, or attempting to deface or damage the furniture or walls as if to deny or destroy the intentions and parameters of the psychotherapeutic experience.

EXPECTATION: All the toys, papers, crayons, puppets, dolls, tables and chairs, and other materials that are needed for the psychotherapy to proceed are available in the office or play area.

It is assumed that most professional offices have the necessary tools to conduct the tasks of the corresponding professions. Psychotherapists' offices or play areas are no exception. Dolls, puppets, and other play objects are essential tools for the child psychotherapist (Bender and Woltmann, 1952; Haworth, 1968; I. E. Shapiro, 1975; Claman, 1980; Cantor and Kestenbaum, 1986). It is nonetheless a common occurrence for a child to bring to, store in, or take out various articles from the therapist's playroom or office. These reactions symbolically challenge the assumption that the feelings and reactions of the therapeutic work can be contained within set limits. They are often best understood as expressions of the child's personal needs that are associated with the therapy sessions and with the therapist.

Some children, for example, may bring to the sessions their own toys or other objects as a means of showing the therapist that they have some value and worth in their own right, which they themselves may doubt. Other children ask to take objects from the play area home with them as an expression and reminder of their accomplishments and feelings during the therapy hour. Others want tangible objects to keep as a reminder of the therapist between sessions. Some children may feel possessive of their relationship with the therapist and want to safeguard it from other children by taking a part of the therapist's store of toys home, in this way sometimes secretly feeling that they are taking a part of the therapist home with them. Some children feel they are insignificant to the therapist and fear they will be forgotten by the time of the next session. They may wish to leave a drawing of theirs on the wall to remind the therapist of their existence between sessions, or they may wish to leave a toy or small car or doll from home as a reminder of themselves to the therapist. These times create many difficult moments. For example, one child may want to hide a favorite toy he or she has used at a session as a means of keeping it away from other children until the next session. Another child may implore the therapist for a favorite toy or other article as a personal gift to take home.

3

Difficult Moments
Remembered

This chapter presents 11 brief narratives provided by senior colleagues who are recognized for their work in psychotherapy with children. We solicited these recollections to provide the reader with what we hope will be a series of interesting examples explaining how others have managed their own most difficult moments. We asked contributors to share with us and with you incidents in their psychotherapeutic work with children that had been memorable for them—in particular, difficult moments that had been especially problematic and how they had been managed or perhaps mismanaged. We also asked them to indicate how the situations or problematic events might have affected them in their work with children.

These examples suggest that difficult moments are part of everyone's career; no one escapes them or feels that he or she has always handled them well. They are often exasperating and frustrating at the time, but in retrospect are often remembered for having been most helpful in the development of the practitioner's own psychotherapeutic skills. They sometimes seem to threaten the entire psychotherapy process, but if handled well may provide a nodal point that allows the therapy to move forward positively. They also point out that variations of approach within accepted principles of psychotherapy are common. Finally, through the challenges and opportunities that difficult moments present, both personally and professionally, they offer the opportunity for growth as individuals and as professionals.

A Difficult-Moment Mother

Paul L. Adams, M.D.

There are some tensions in our human existence that are never resolved: separation vs. fusion, narcissism vs. altruism, militancy vs. nonviolence, parents vs. children. As my professional life in child psychotherapy has gone along, the dialectic that I came to call my own and that I now tell about has centered mainly on parent vs. child.

Work with the parent(s) of a child with a mental disorder often shows us how little can be done, but work without a parent usually demonstrates that *nothing* can be done. The parent can be salutary *or* unhealthy—noxious, obstructive, subversive, disdainful, and the rest—*or* nonsalient to a child's psychotherapy and outside of therapy. Overall, the gratifying surprise about parents is that so many do have such reservoirs and caches of reasonableness and helping empathy that await our discovery and reinforcement in their relationship to their children. Vocally antichild parents may surprise us with their barely dormant compassion, identification, and altruism respecting their child, our patient. As their nonpossessive guardianship of the child unfolds, joy arises in all corners.

My professional career with families has convinced me that the Fourth Commandment ("Honor thy father and mother that thy days may be long on the earth") is pernicious for both children and parents. Under the Fourth Commandment's injunction, too much impetus is given to parental distortions of splitting, projective identification, role reversal, narcissistic identification, identification with the aggressor— and to parental practices of neglect, physical abuse, sexual molestation, mental abuse, brainwashing, and persecutory behavior. As a psychotherapist, I continue to learn how bad parenting sometimes comes to be. I am ill-disposed toward the notion that children must fearfully "honor" their parents in order to survive and feel fully human.

I am a child advocate, as well as a healer and teacher, whenever my professional role as a psychotherapist is effective. As a child advocate, I often have occasion to strengthen parents in *their* advocacy of their child's welfare in the school, court, and, yes, in the home. As a child advocate, I try to negotiate a better position, a better-lived life, for the individual child as well as for children generally. This task is not easy in a society obsessed with violent war, practicing corporal punishment, and stripping children of their rights to be free and to be protected and served well. Always there are intrafamilial tensions to be balanced and understood and, once in awhile, to be made explicit, resolved, and muted in reconciliation.

Some things work while others do not. A body of tactics is formed as we practice child psychotherapy, and modi operandi take shape and become our usual ways of going about our work with children and their parents.

My Usual Procedure with Parents

It has proven effective, so I usually first see the parents, without the child and preparatory to my initial session with the child. We explore conjugal relations, discuss parental roles, talk about families of origin, and bring out and underline personal traits. I get a look into the marriage, the pregnancy with this child (and others), the self-image of each parent, and where strengths and weaknesses lie. I determine what family secrets there are, which ones are to be kept from the child, and even whether either parent would wish a tête-á-tête session with me. I get the development story of the child and the parents' view of the history of the present illness, and I ask each parent to tell me something he or she feels to be very good about the child I am to see. I probe for parental empathy by asking what each thinks the child is trying to tell his or her interpersonal world, asking each to see the family from the child's perspective—"through the child's eyes." I caution them that I am a child advocate and hence will respect the child and, once I get going with the child, will not want to have contact with either parent *unless the child is present*. I ask them to explain my stand to the child before I interview him or her, reemphasizing the need for the parents to come clean during these early sessions, because later they will be seen as auxiliaries of the child. With that overall plan, I am usually ready to see the child, who will by now be prepared to see me.

A Mother Planted in the Doorway

I had seen the mother (only) of Jonathan, an 8-year-old hyperactive boy, on two occasions, prior to seeing the mother and stepfather on one visit. Then I saw Jonathan alone for one visit, and at that time I asked that both his parents and his little half-sister be there to join us a half hour into my second session with him. They did, and the session seemed to go well. At the time of my *third* session with Jonathan, when I called to him in the waiting room, his mother hopped up and planted herself in the doorway of the consulting room. She demanded a private talk with me before I saw her boy Jonathan.

The element of surprise lay in her effort to break the agreement we had made—that I'd not meet with her, or the stepfather, without Jonathan. This was a mother who had divorced her first husband even though it meant she would be impoverished immediately. Before marrying again—her present husband—she had weathered life as a single mother and, during her own period of introspection and self-knowl- edge, had dropped the religion of her parents (Christianity) to embrace a religion of her own (one of the world's major non-Christian religions). I respected her valor, her autono- my, and her having obtained by her own efforts her training in what I regarded as a noble health profession. So to see her discard the rapport that I had believed to exist between us was shocking. Her moral and interpersonal jujitsu threw me, too.

I said, "But we agreed to meet only when Jonathan was present."

Thereupon she told me, "But I question that. Besides, I have several other bones to pick with you."

Jonathan had stood up to watch the fight and remained standing, which gave me some courage. I insisted on a few minutes with Jonathan alone. The boy walked toward the consulting room.

In the office, I explained to Jonathan, "I prefer not to talk with parents behind a boy's back," trying to be bureaucratic, business-as-usual, and general-rule about my policy.

His comment was, "My mom and dad think I have too much fun here."

Jonathan and I talked about my unwillingness to give his mother either (1) a talk between her and me without Jonathan or (2) time (even with Jonathan) at the very beginning of the session. I tried to explain that by seeing him first, I could keep better focused on him and, furthermore, that he and I could formulate an agenda of what needed to be dealt with when his mother joined us later in the session. Jonathan seemed to take heart both that he and I were together and that I did not take orders from his mother. We mapped out an agenda: Talk about the "too much fun here," the stimulant medication I had prescribed, the impending school visit, and an allowance for Jonathan. As soon as I elicited his preliminary views on each topic, I summoned his mother.

Our agenda meant nothing to Jonathan's mother. She launched into a tirade against me as a therapist: "My husband and I want to stop this. The medicine does help, but talking with you is worthless to us because you have no understanding of our values or of our life-style. Two things make that very clear—the allowance and the meals." She referred to my asking the parents where they stood on giving Jonathan an allowance and if there were any times, such as at mealtime, when parents and children were all together. To ask about a topic was to criticize or command Jonathan's mother. Although her husband held to a hard line on never sparing the rod, a virtue that he attributed to his Central European mother, mother and stepfather presided jointly over a chaotic household in which the dust was settled, occasionally and briefly, by a show of parental force. They had no order, no regular meals, no true discipline or discipleship. To them, an allowance was a bonus to an undeserving child. They believed the child would get the wrong message from being "rewarded" without hard travail to show that he was deserving of money. I explained that I was *inquiring* about times together and an allowance, not to require them but simply to find out.

After that, things went better between parents and therapist and, amazingly enough, between parents and Jonathan.

"Schmako Says"

Jules Bemporad, M.D.

As luck would have it, the most awkward situation in child psychotherapy with which I have had to deal occurred only a few months after I started my child training. I had been assigned an 8-year-old boy who presented with hyperactivity, inappropriate and clownish behavior in school, social and peer problems, and urinary frequency—all in the face of outstanding academic achievement. History revealed a host of interesting, if somewhat outlandish, facts. The parents complained that the patient often paraded naked and liked to expose or play with his penis in front of them, all the while giggling hysterically. He also had developed a fetish for his mother's feet, attempting to lick them or rub them while fondling his genitalia. His father exhibited numerous oddities, the most striking of which was his use of one of the two bedrooms in their apartment for his "museum," in which he stored old paper bags, pieces of string, old pencils, and other "collectibles," all in an exact order. A malignant aspect of this obsession was that the father blamed and beat the patient if any of the articles had been disturbed. The mother appeared as a limited, immature woman who still depended greatly on her own mother and who inappropriately used the patient as a companion so as to discourage activities outside the house.

In therapy, the boy related well, as if welcoming an extrafamilial relationship. He demonstrated impressive intelligence and a precocious ability to recount and make up stories. Eventually, he shared with the therapist a fantasy world that he had constructed and that was inhabited by feet—and still later, a more personal world inhabited by penises. He was quite aware that these fantasy worlds were his mental creations, and reality-testing remained intact. However, he enjoyed making endless drawings of this enchanted world, which he called "Schmakoland," in which "Schmakos" (probably a derivation of "schmuck"), or detached penises, went through everyday activities. In this phase of therapy, he began talking about his own "Schmako," saying that he loved it, that he "adored it," and that he liked it better than he liked his mother. He also invented a game "Schmako Says. . .," in which he played two parts: one part of the penis that commanded him to perform acts (e.g., take two steps forward or backward, sit down, stand up) and the other part of himself obeying these directions. At times, while executing his drawings of "Schmakoland," he would start laughing and grab his genital area in a mocking fashion.

On one such occasion, he cried out, "I love my Schmako," and proceeded to unzip his pants and pull out his penis. Although from the progression of the clinical material thus far, I should have been prepared for his eventually exhibiting himself, I was quite apprehensive and did not know how to react to this turn of events. For lack of anything better to do, and to quell my own anxiety, I decided to resort to the old maxim of "when in doubt analyze." With studied calm, I asked him why he had pulled out his Schmako, to which he replied that he adored it and wanted me to see it, all with a great deal of malicious laughter. I replied that I had now seen his Schmako and he could put it back in his pants, to which he responded with even more giggling, but did comply with my request. He then proceeded to laugh and sing "I love my Schmako" loudly, running around the office, then collapsing to the floor exhausted. The remainder of the session consisted of his making drawings of "Schmakoland" in his usual relaxed manner.

In discussions of the session with my supervisor, we both speculated that my patient's need to exhibit himself represented some significant psychodynamic relating to castration fears and the requirement for reassurance of bodily integrity as well as some sort of defiance toward the therapist, who had taken on the feared and hated qualities of the father. However, we agreed, much to my relief, that as pressing as these needs might be, therapy had to represent the mores of society and further acts of exhibitionism were to be firmly discouraged. In the subsequent sessions, the patient did announce that he was going to show me his Schmako in a teasing, threatening manner—an announcement to which I responded by stating flatly that such behavior was not allowed in therapy any more than it was outside the office and that he might tell me, if he liked, why he wished to exhibit himself, but was not to actually do it.

It is to the credit of the patient's ingenuity that he devised a way to "shock" me with his Schmako while conforming to the imposed restrictions of therapy. He began to hand me pieces of paper that had been folded over and over and that I was to unfold. At each unfolding was a statement about the Schmako, culminating in a large drawing of a penis when the paper was totally unfolded. When I got to this last step, he would start laughing and rolling on the floor, obviously satisfied that he had put one over on me. In time, therapy moved on to other themes.

Although this patient did relatively well, I am not quite sure, in retrospect, that we chose the most therapeutic option. It later emerged that the patient's fascination with Schmakoland was a way of dealing with his mother's frankly seductive behavior, his father's jealousy of her behavior, and his inability to escape the situation. The father had actually threatened to cut off the boy's penis. As if to reinforce the real possibility that he would carry out his threat, he had told the boy, as they were passing a delicatessen, that the salamis and other cold cuts were actually penises that had been cut off. The patient seemed to have invented Schmakoland as a way of ensuring the survival of his penis, even after it had been severed. My supervisor and I had come to the correct interpretations of the exhibitionism, even if we had not anticipated such a brutal basis for the psychodynamics.

Perhaps, though, we should have respected the patient's need to demonstrate his integrity and to defy the father via the transference to the therapist, who, it is to be hoped, would have reacted in a less competitive and more benevolent manner. It might have been better to allow the patient to expose himself and to react to his Schmako in a very matter-of-fact manner so as to convey the message that his masculinity or sexuality was not so threatening, so powerful, or so dangerous. This would have allowed a more rapid emergence of other material, a closer working alliance, and one less instance of confirming for the patient that his sexuality was inappropriate and disturbing. Thanks to this particular patient's outstanding imagination, he managed to represent the same issue via drawings, which we smugly termed "sublimation." Obviously, not all 8-year-olds are capable of this creative shift.

I do not relate this case history to suggest that we should condone such grossly egregious behavior in psychotherapy with children. Rather, my concern is that we not discourage or squelch nondangerous behavior on the basis of our own discomfort or simply of social convention as it emerges, but rather that we understand its meaning in terms of the therapeutic context.

A Terror in the Playroom

Irving N. Berlin, M.D.

I was asked to see Timmy, age 6, because he had become unmanageable at home and at school. Since the birth of a sister a year ago, Timmy had become assaultive toward children in his kindergarten and first-grade classes, smashed his desk, torn books into shreds, and hit any child within range with his ruler or notebook. When he stabbed a child with a pencil, he was expelled from school. At home, he tried to knock over his sister's crib and to strike her when she was in his mother's arms. He also struck his mother when he could. He did not strike his father, who spanked him several times for hitting his mother or the baby. Spanking did not alter his violent behavior. Timmy also destroyed all the furniture in his room when he was locked up as punishment. Because of his father's stern interdiction, Timmy rarely destroyed anything in other parts of the house.

When I saw Timmy for the first time, I took him by the hand into the playroom and explained what I knew about his coming to see me, without any response from him. He continued in his silent, sullen demeanor as I explained the rules of the playroom and then showed him the various toys, dolls, blocks, and drawing materials, inviting him to use whichever materials he wished to. When I let go of his hand after conducting the tour of the playroom, he picked up a block and threw it at me, not very hard. I firmly reminded him that he could not hurt me or himself, and I would not permit him to break anything, whereupon he picked up a wooden truck, quickly smashed it to the floor, and stomped on it, destroying it. I commented on his anger toward both his sister and adults and told him that I intended to set limits. I would grab him and hold him the next time he tried to break anything.

No sooner were the words out of my mouth than he grabbed a wooden helicopter. I grabbed him, took the helicopter away, and proceeded to hold him so that he could not hit or kick me. He banged his head on my chest, obviously trying to butt me in the face. I commented that I would hold him until he could control himself. He then began to scream, over and over, in a deafening voice, "Help, I'm being killed."

Despite my soundproofed door, I was sure his parents and others in my waiting room could hear. Feeling a bit embarrassed at all the noise, I shouted back, "Oh, shut up."

Timmy looked startled and stopped his yelling for a few moments. Since his bodily tension did not ease during the rest of the interminably long hour, I continued to hold him tightly. He resumed his yelling, although not quite so loudly as before. At the end of the hour, I held on to his hand and firmly walked him to his parents in the waiting room, not feeling terribly effective. To my comment, "See you next week," he spat out, "Not on your life, you bastard." My face turned red and I escorted my next patient, a very quiet, obsessive little girl, into the playroom.

Having dealt with a number of hostile, destructive children who required initial restraint in the playroom, I knew

Timmy was going to be difficult and exhausting. I arranged to see him once a week and both parents every other week.

The following week, I took Timmy firmly by the hand and we entered the playroom. As I turned to close the door, he broke free of my grasp, ran to the toy shelf, and swept all the toys within reach to the floor. I grabbed him and quickly restrained him. As he lay loudly screaming invectives, I began to talk very softly about how much it hurt to have a baby take his place in his parents' hearts. It must seem like they don't love him any more. I could understand why he felt so mad at everyone. Very slowly, his loud shouting became a quiet protest, and he could hear my repeated statements about my understanding of his problems. He relaxed a bit in my arms, but not enough for me to release even a hand. As we left the playroom this time, he was quieter and only grunted when I said we would meet again next week.

The following week, we again went into the playroom hand in hand. I made sure I had a firm hold on his hand as I closed the door. We stood looking at each other. I asked him what he'd like to do. Did he need me to hold him? He suddenly kicked me and punched me above my right eye, cutting the skin. I was in pain and the cut was bleeding copiously into my eye. Timmy looked terrified. I grabbed him with one hand and with the other tried to stem the flow of blood with my handkerchief. Timmy lay quietly, making no effort to escape my one-handed grip on both his hands. I let my anger and hurt be heard in my voice as I screamed how much I hurt, that I was so mad I would like to slug him, but I would try just to hold him and not hurt him.

Over and over, I let him hear how I felt. As the bleeding stopped and the pain receded, my voice became calmer. I told him that I had been scared I might hurt him because I was so angry and hurt so much. I was glad I could control myself and not hurt him. Timmy's face slowly regained color as my

voice became calmer. We both lay on the floor and I restrained his hands and feet, holding him not quite as tightly
as before. I continued to tell him that although I wasn't sure
he meant to hurt me and make me bleed, he was nevertheless
the one who had thrown the block. Several times toward the
end of the hour, and again at the door as we left the playroom, he very softly said, "I'm sorry." I said nothing to his
parents about the events in the playroom.

Next week, the fourth session, Timmy put his hand in
mine as we entered the playroom and waited quietly until I
closed the door. When I asked him what he would like to do,
he led me to the dollhouse. I released his arm, keeping a
vigilant eye on him. He also watched me carefully. He began
to place various dolls representing his family into various
rooms of the dollhouse. He found a fire truck and proceeded
to run it over the mother, father, baby, and a girl doll, but not
the boy doll. Then he dropped them from their rooms on the
second floor of the house. Each time he ran the truck over a
family member, he looked at me with some apprehension. To
my repeated comments, "You sure fixed that one, it probably
couldn't be fixed even by the doctor," he would nod and then
return to repeatedly running over each doll, leaning on the
fire truck to make sure they were run over hard. At the end of
the hour, he put the truck away and placed the dolls in the
dollhouse. He nodded as I commented, "See you next
week."

I heard from Timmy's parents in their regular, twice-
monthly session that the previous week had been quieter and
the least hostile they could remember. In the previous session, I had tried to help his mother be clear and firm with him
and to act promptly by sending him to his room for a "time-
out" when he became even a bit violent so that there would
be no major escalation of violence.

When Timmy hurt me and saw the blood flow, it became

clear he was in terror that his death wishes toward his baby sister and parents, which drove his violence toward others, might result in terrible retribution. He feared that he might be severely injured or even killed for injuring me. My loud and angry comments were very scary. He did not appear reassured by my comment that I would try not to hurt him. After it became clear that he was safe, he lived through terrible moments of fear of revenge being visited on him for his death wished toward his sister, his mother, and probably his father. When the terrible retribution did not occur, and he found himself unhurt, his massive anxiety and anger were reduced. He could begin to express his conflicts in fantasy play rather than in acting-out behaviors.

In subsequent sessions, Timmy played out various scenarios, destroying his family or part of it, always including his baby sister and at least one parent. With nods, he acknowledged my speculations about his pain at being replaced by his sister as his parent's favorite. After injuring the doll representing his sister or parent, he eventually became the rescuing doctor who repaired the damage. With pride, he would declare, "See, all fixed. Pretty good, huh?" I praised his efforts as a doctor and continued my comments, understanding his hurt, sad, and angry feelings, but insisting that he could not continue hurting people because he was hurt and angry.

Timmy's fantasy play also led to his expressing some of his fears that to be loved he would have to be a girl, without a penis. With help, his parents were able to both control and engage him in play. His dad could roughhouse with him, making clear that this was an activity only for boys. He came to one session feeling proud that he and his dad had penises.

The essential issue is how an accidental event can be turned into a therapeutic experience. The therapist must have repeated experiences to learn that under certain circumstances, his or her feelings should be expressed. In seeing them expressed, the child sees that strong feelings need not lead to destructive or assaultive action. Also, it becomes important that the therapist not pretend to be unhurt but, despite the hurt, try not to be revengeful and retaliatory. Thus, both child and therapist have a new therapeutic experience.

The Soiled Charmer

Norbert B. Enzer, M.D.

Ruthie was 6 years old at the time and doing reasonably well in the first grade. She was the middle child of three girls. Her parents, the father a veterinarian, and the mother formerly a physical therapist, had brought her to me because of secondary encopresis, which they had tried to manage with the help of the family pediatrician for about one year. Ruthie seemed to have little concern about the symptom, played well with peers, and was described by her parents as being for the most part a cheery and rather remarkably cooperative child at home and at school. With the exception of the soiling, Ruthie had been much less of a concern to her parents than her older sister, who was portrayed as an irritable, demanding, but highly competent 9-year-old. She teased Ruthie "unmercifully" not only about the soiling, but also about almost anything Ruthie did or did not do. This pattern antedated the onset of Ruthie's symptom. The younger sister, age 4½, was described by the parents with joy and virtually unlimited satisfaction. She was said to have a "magnetic personality."

In retrospect, although they had seen Ruthie as a love-able and pleasant child, the parents acknowledged that of the three girls, she probably received the least attention; she seemed to demand less than her older sister and was not as engaging as the younger one. Often, she seemed quite content to play alone. Her mother admitted that it was likely that she asked more of Ruthie in regard to simple household chores, since Ruthie was so much more likely to respond positively than her older sister. More specifically, both parents were aware that during the past year, they were less likely to "hug" Ruthie; that they frequently questioned her about soiling; that positive interactions with her were less frequent, in part because of a behavior–management plan developed with the aid of the pediatrician; and that there had been some harsh verbal exchanges with her.

Ruthie was an appealing child. Her interactions with me belied her age. She entered into play therapy easily. Her mother reported after the first couple of sessions that Ruthie truly seemed to look forward to the visits. Initially very organized, her play involved the preparation of imaginary food for tea parties or picnics to which I was invited. She was a "perfect hostess." She seemed to have a rather unusual sense of time and would clean up the playroom with little comment from me when she noticed by the clock in the room that the end of a session was approaching. After several similar sessions in which conversations associated with the "meals" involved topics of adult interests, what I thought about a recent concert, or the previous evening's television news, Ruthie began to play with the dollhouse and the doll family, activities that largely excluded me. She would converse among the doll family and would respond to my questions or comments, but I was not invited to participate in the tea parties or picnics as I had been before. In the play itself, there were frequent quarrels among the children and between the parents or other adults and the children. At times, it appeared that the children and the adults operated in quite separate environments that would periodically conflict with one another. Frequently, one doll, usually a child, was somehow isolated and Ruthie would describe the feelings of this doll as either gladness in not being involved in a controversy or loneliness.

The eleventh session began very differently than had any before. Rather than promptly going to the toys, Ruthie stood silently and rather uncomfortably in the center of the playroom for a couple of minutes, then moved very close to the arm of the chair in which I had seated myself. I commented that she "seemed different today," and she replied that she did not feel like playing and put her hand on my arm. I was aware of a fecal odor that I had not noticed in any previous session. In previous sessions, we had talked about the symptom of soiling as the reason her parents had asked me to help her. On those occasions when it was discussed, she had tried to avoid the subject, claimed the soiling did not "bother" her, and said directly that she did not want to talk about it. As she stood near me, still touching my arm, she asked if I had heard the joke about "the polka-dot gorilla." "Why did the gorilla have polka dots?," she asked, with a broad but seemingly forced smile. When I admitted my ignorance, she supplied, "Because they ran out of plain colors at the gorilla factory," laughed loudly, and skipped away a couple of steps. A moment later, she suddenly sat down astride my outstretched legs still forcing a smile.

I was startled by Ruthie's rather bold action and felt a sudden impulse to pull my legs out from under her. I was very aware that my trousers might be stained by fecal matter through Ruthie's thin shorts. "Was that a funny joke?," she asked, rocking slowly back and forth. My discomfort intensified as I recognized the sexual implications. I dismissed my desire to move my legs or to simply reach down and lift her from her squatting position. When I said that I was not sure I understood the joke, she ceased the rocking movements and began to suck her index finger, a behavior I had not seen before but one the parents had reported to occur when she was "tired." Hugging herself with her other arm, she stared at me with a plaintive expression as we both remained motionless for perhaps several minutes. It felt as if each of us were trying to find a way of extricating ourselves from the situation. Nothing that crossed my mind in those moments seemed appropriate, and I remained silent.

Ruthie interrupted the impasse. She stood up, still sucking her finger, moved to the window, and quietly gazed outside. With her back to me, she said softly, after a couple of minutes "I can't stay so long today. I have to go home."

I thought she might be crying, but when she turned to me, I saw that she was not. Still trying to regain my composure, I said, clumsily, "Right now?"

"Yes," she replied, moving toward the door.

I wanted to find something to say that would allow her to remain. "Maybe we should talk about why you are uncomfortable," I said. She glanced at me blankly and opened the door to leave, but said nothing. We walked to the waiting room in silence.

Her mother was surprised to see us, but had been forewarned weeks earlier that Ruthie might want to leave some sessions early. I told her that Ruthie said she "has to go home." Taking Ruthie's hand, the mother said, "Okay, we'll see you next time."

Several hours later, the mother called to apologize for Ruthie's premature departure. However, knowing nothing more about the earlier events, she said Ruthie had told her on the way home in the car that she had "an accident" in her pants and was embarrassed. The mother said this was the first time Ruthie had made any such acknowledgment or voluntarily interrupted any activity. As a result, she could see some positive features. I thanked her but added nothing more.

The next session again began with Ruthie standing uncomfortably in the middle of the playroom. "My mother said I should tell you that I didn't want to come today," she said with her head down. Feeling I wanted to be supportive, which in retrospect may have been intended as much to ease my discomfort as to ease Ruthie's, I said, "That happens sometimes," and added, "I'm glad you decided to come."

After a few moments, Ruthie *asked* if she could play with the dollhouse and spent the rest of the session arranging furniture and placing the dolls in the proper locations, but engaging them in little action. My attempts to turn the conversation to her reluctance to come to the session or to the events of the week before were unsuccessful, and it was not until a month later that we were able to productively discuss the interchanges that had made both of us so uncomfortable.

Comment

Ruthie continued in therapy and did well. Whether this particular episode ultimately influenced the course of therapy can be considered only hypothetically, but I did not handle it well. It was truly a first and, thankfully, a last.

I have seen many children with encopresis and have been aware that occasionally they have soiled before or during sessions. I have had young children, of both sexes, sit down across my legs and even rock themselves. Either behavior alone might not have caused me so much trouble, but together they provoked an unqualified desire to get out of a very unpleasant situation, and yet I felt if I did what came to mind, it would jeopardize such alliance as had developed at the time. I felt immobilized and inadequate. It is a credit to Ruthie that she managed to deal with the situation as well as she did.

I frequently tell supervisees that it is sometimes best to do nothing. What I usually intend by such a comment is that an elective decision to do or say nothing can be highly appropriate. The situation was one in which it was not so much that I had made a decision as that I had been caught "off guard," badly. I was so startled by Ruthie's sitting down across my legs and so concerned for myself—more correctly, for my clothing—that I was unable to see the significance of her behavior in context or to respond for her. What crossed my mind were alternatives to protect myself rather than to deal with her behaviors and feelings.

As I thought about this episode initially, I focused on my reactions to Ruthie's act of sitting across my legs. My responses, or lack of more appropriate alternatives, were disquieting to me. What became apparent was that I had missed some critical aspects of the context. For a couple of weeks prior to this session, Ruthie had taken my hand, at least briefly, as we walked between the waiting room and the playroom at the beginning or end of a session, a gesture that I essentially ignored, perhaps even deliberately, because it occurred in the "public" hallway. Her activities in the playroom had remained mostly unchanged except that on two occasions she had mentioned, almost in passing, conflicts at home with her older sister and her mother. My responses were intended to explore the circumstances of the conflicts and her feelings about them, but each time she avoided pursuing these matters. I had not responded to the meaning of these behaviors in the relationship between Ruthie and me, either the reaching out for physical contact or the overture of presenting a real-life problem for the first time.

When we were able to discuss Ruthie's behavior in the

particular session, it became clear that it had several meanings and that it was motivated by several forces. Her coming close to my chair and touching my arm were expressions of her desire for closeness and an attempt to alter the previous pattern of our relationship. Her previous attempts, admittedly subtle, had been largely ignored or avoided. The soiling, which apparently occurred after we entered the playroom, was probably related as much to her apprehension about her positive feelings as to anything, although she also clearly knew that soiling was more likely to result in rejection than closeness. The silly joke could be seen as her attempt to "defuse" or deny her feelings. She later acknowledged that she feared I would reject her overture again, but she saw that possibility as the result of the soiling. Sitting on my legs, sucking her finger, and rocking were regressive testing behaviors that after a few moments, she herself recognized as inappropriate. There were affiliative and hostile, as well as sexual, aspects to the behavior. In retrospect, she too was concerned that our relationship might be damaged, but she did what she had to do at that moment—she got out! Interestingly, she later expressed her awareness of my discomfort and, even later, described her disappointment and even anger at my lack of sensitivity and my failure to respond more helpfully. Although she denied any such feeling, it seemed to me she felt that I had abandoned her in those few difficult moments weeks earlier.

As I have thought about this situation and discussed it with trainees and others, a variety of alternatives to my actual behavior have occurred. Obviously, there is no way of knowing how different responses on my part might have influenced the series of events or the subsequent therapy.

Leaving aside the possibility that had I responded differently to Ruthie in previous sessions, the events of the particular session might not have occurred, one might wonder what would have happened if I had responded more positively in the first few minutes of the session. Rather than the neutral comment that she seemed "different" as she moved close to me, I might have said, "It is nice to see you," or I might have simply covered her hand with mine as she touched my arm. Rather than responding to her joke neutrally, I might have said that I could see she was trying to give us both a good laugh, or that it is fun to laugh at something together, or simply that she seemed to enjoy it. I might even have offered an interpretation that sometimes people try to laugh when they really have feelings that are serious or troublesome.

After Ruthie squatted across my legs, my inaction seemed particularly problematic. I might have moved, even stood up, thus simply physically extricating both of us. I might have verbally acknowledged my discomfort, perhaps directing her to some other activity. I might have suggested that she seemed to want to be close to me that day, maybe suggesting that we could sit together on the floor. The point is, there were alternatives, and some might have been more helpful than inaction. Even after Ruthie had declared her intention to leave, there was the possibility of a different outcome. I might have acknowledged her discomfort or even said, "I am sorry you feel you have to leave," perhaps adding that I had been looking forward to seeing her. Had I been more empathic, I might have suggested that it seemed as though she felt I had disappointed her.

At almost every point, there were alternative actions that might have changed the situation or its outcome. The "bottom line" in this situation would seem to be that I did not recognize, or I denied, Ruthie's desire for closeness. Countertransference surely played a part, perhaps a large part, in my reactions. Ruthie was an appealing child, but she also had a most unpleasant symptom. Retrospective consideration of alternatives can be helpful, but so can introspection and discussions with others, even for more experienced therapists.

The Magic Circle

Clarice J. Kestenbaum, M.D.

Charles A. was referred for analytic therapy by the nursery-school principal because of immaturity, antisocial classroom behavior, and "for being a really sad kid." When I first saw Charles in consultation, he was a tall, well-developed, good-looking 5½-year-old boy whose messy long blond hair kept falling into his eyes. He never used a handkerchief, and his smeared face and occasional grimaces detracted from his overall appearance. He appeared younger than his age because of a number of infantilisms in speech and manner. The immature behavior—clinging and whining—disappeared the moment his mother left the room.

Charles's father was a successful professional who seemed to be at his wit's end when confronted with his son's school behavior. Mrs. A. was an only child of a wealthy industrialist. A brilliant student, she now worked for a prestigious law firm. She had never wanted children, admitting that "this is the only one I'll have." She was depressed about the nursery principal's report, being herself highly perfectionist and judgmental. She (also) denied that any problems were Charles's, blaming the school, the teacher, and other children. She drank heavily but denied being an alcoholic. Both parents admitted that their marriage was in trouble, but neither one "believed in therapy or counseling."

Mr. and Mrs. A. told me that the first indication that anything was wrong was a nursery-school report on 3-year-old Charles stating that he lacked confidence, made no attempt to do new things, and was easily frustrated, giving up without trying. Mrs. A. did recall that as an infant he had been hypersensitive to noise and fearful in the presence of strangers. Until age 3, moreover, he sucked his fingers continually and wouldn't leave the house without his favorite pillow. His classmates teased him for crying and for having tantrums; his teacher reported that he occasionally lost control and struck children and even adults. A psychological test had been performed prior to the consultation—the full-scale I.Q. was 112. The T.A.T. responses were full of punitive and retaliatory comments: "In this picture the boy is killed and that's all, because Jesus killed him and you know why? Because he didn't say grace after lunch."

I considered Charles to be developmentally immature, a depressed child who "gave up" in the face of perfectionist parental demands. I recommended psychoanalytically oriented psychotherapy, a low-pressure, structured first grade with small classes and sensitive teachers, and weekly parental counseling. Mrs. A. rarely came to the sessions and seemed bored by the entire process.

In his first therapy session, Charles acted out a story with hand puppets, a scene that appeared and reappeared many times. A baby tiger, 5 years old, runs away from his forest cave "because his daddy spanks him and his mother leaves him with a baby-sitter. He hates school and wants to hide in his own cave and never come out. He has no friends. He is always scared." The play sessions that followed dealt with similar themes. Charles spent many hours preoccupied with Legos and blocks and constructed castles that were safe, "with a very strong base." He rarely spoke about problems at home or school; he usually responded to my occasional questions with the comment, "No more talk. I won't tell you how I feel. Shut up."

After several months of therapy, Charles's school reports improved. He had settled into a new school environment in which the principal was warm and motherly, yet firm and able to set limits. Charles was soon able to join a group, started to participate in activities, and began to read with comprehension and pleasure. Six months after beginning treatment, he was involved in a very positive therapeutic relationship. He spoke more about his past problems. One remark was: "There is a bad kid Stevie who makes a lot of noise and has to leave the room."

"Maybe he has a problem like the one you used to have a long time ago," I suggested.

"Yes," he replied, "I used to have that problem, but that was in the other school. It went away."

Therapy had been progressing smoothly for 6 months when one afternoon at 3 o'clock, Mrs. A. appeared in my office without an appointment, dragging a frightened Charles by one arm. "Since coming, her son Charles has become obnoxious," she began. "He uses vulgar expressions and curses. Yesterday he made a disgusting sign with his finger. I'm warning you [she shook her finger at Charles but looked directly at me while she spoke], if you say even one more curse word you're never coming back here again."

Fortunately, my 3 o'clock patient had not yet arrived. I led Charles into the consulting room and asked Mrs. A. to leave the room. Charles was upset and began to cry. I kneeled beside him so our eyes were on the same level. "Listen, Charles," I said, "you heard what your mother said, and it sounds like she means business. Some grown-ups can't stand curses, even though you and I know they're only words and can't hurt anyone."

"Yeah, like throwing rocks at Billy or hitting Mary" [last year's playground activities].

"That's right," I agreed. "So even though you're only a little boy—six is really too young to tell you what I'm going to tell you now—I think you're grown up enough to understand: Outside—at home or in the shopping center or at school—you are not allowed to use curse words, but here, in this office, we'll pretend we have a magic circle surrounding the room."

Charles ran around the perimeter of the room, touching the walls, the windows, the door.

"Yes, in here, in this special space, we can say anything. . . . even 'shit'!" he asked quietly.

"Yes, 'shit' is O.K."

"And 'asshole'?"

"Yes."

"And the F word?" he whispered gravely.

"Yes, even that. We can pretend the puppets and dolls are talking and they can say anything they like. The characters in our stories can say or do anything they like."

Charles tried out the new rules with evident glee.

"But," I said, slowly meeting his gaze, "if you say these curse words at home—even one more time—mother won't let you come back here any more. I know you like to come and we have a good time [and learn about your worries and work out your problems], but if your mother and your dad"—"He always does what she says," Charles interrupted. "Anyway," I continued, "you heard what she said, and she usually keeps her word. I can help you with most of your problems, but I can't help you with everything. You have to be able to use self-control and do it all by yourself. Can you do that?" Charles nodded and we left the room.

It seemed clear to me that Mrs. A. was trying to find a rationale for discontinuing therapy, particularly since Charles had been making significant academic social progress at school. I had never been able to establish much of an alliance with her, and her husband didn't want to "make waves." They refused to see the therapist I had recommended for them. I therefore chose to deal with the reality of Charles's life. I had no power over his parents; I had to present the facts and hope he could use enough control to modify his behavior. Obviously, he could not have done so if he had been an impulsive, hyperactive, or borderline psychotic child, but I thought he could most likely comply with the rules.

I saw Charles at his regular appointed time, and then for a subsequent session, and (take one session at a time, I thought), another and another—in fact, for 2 years. Charles cursed up a storm in the office for several weeks—with great enthusiasm—but never once overstepped the boundaries at home. I complimented him for his exceptional control on numerous occasions and used his ability to exercise self-restraint as an example of how he could do anything he wanted once he made up his mind. He rarely gave up in the face of failure in school and proceeded on a normal developmental track thenceforth. Several years after termination, I actually received a thank-you note from his parents.

The Balcony

Melvin Lewis, M.D.

One late afternoon in the fall some years ago, I was seeing John, a 10-year-old boy who had been referred with the symptom of risk-taking behavior. John's symptoms began after the tragic drowning of his younger brother, who had fallen from a high seawall near their house.

In previous hours, John had been provocative and destructive, necessitating my seeing him in a playroom, located on the second floor, that was essentially bare except for some heavy office furniture—desk, chairs, easel, and table. The usual smaller play items were stored in a locked cupboard. On this occasion, he was particularly excited and provocative and soon began to edge toward the floor-to-ceiling vertical folding window, which was open and led out to a small balcony. I became concerned and asked him to come away from the window. He saw this as an opportunity for further provocative behavior, however, and began shifting the heavy furniture to form a barricade between us. Since he did not respond to my requests to move away from the window, I began to thread my way between the furniture, trying to get between him and the window. He immediately understood what I was trying to do and seized the opportunity to race out onto the balcony.

By now I was becoming very concerned. I stepped toward him so that I would be able to stop him from going dangerously close to the balcony rail. Suddenly, John, who by this time was thoroughly enjoying what was for him evidently a dangerous and exciting game, reversed his direction, climbed over the furniture, and ran out of the playroom, slamming the door shut behind him. I immediately began to follow him, only to find that the door not only had slammed shut but also had locked and could not be opened. I was now locked inside, and he was free outside the playroom.

I called to John, asking him to open the door, but he made no reply. I then returned to the balcony, hoping to call to someone for help. Unfortunately, most of my colleagues had left the building for the day. The balcony overlooked a pleasant lawn shared with the adult psychiatric hospital ward that at the time was housed in the adjacent building. A few people occasionally used the lawn for lunch, but at this time of day there was no one to be seen. Finally, a young man emerged from another building and began to cross the lawn. I called to him for help, explaining that I had been locked in my room and couldn't get out. The young man looked at me, then glanced at the location of the window, and clearly concluded that I was a psychiatric patient trying to escape from a locked room. He shook his head as if to say "No way" and steadfastly went on his way.

The evening light was now fading, and I knew there would be little chance of anyone else's coming by on the lawn. I returned to the locked door and again called for help, this time banging on the door to attract attention. After what seemed an interminable wait, a maintenance man finally came and set about trying to open the door. He had no luck. The lock had jammed. He then had to call for further assistance. Eventually, he was able to open (or rather remove) the door by unscrewing the hinges.

As I emerged from the office through the open doorway, I found my patient, sitting quietly and watching the whole scene. He seemed partly concerned and partly pleased. Apparently, he had not left the spot from the moment he had run out of the room.

I told John I had been worried about him and asked him to come back into the now open room so that we could talk about what had just happened. He was now cooperative and calm, and we proceeded to experience our best hour together. He told me about his feelings during his excited and agitated behavior earlier in the hour and began to recall similar feelings as he remembered the last time he had played with his brother. He spontaneously recalled how his brother had moved dangerously close to the high seawall when they were playing together. He had been unable to prevent his brother from falling from the seawall or to rescue him. John had felt enormously guilty afterward and subsequently had tried desperately to rid himself of the feeling of guilt as well as to punish himself. He said he had wished over and over that it had all come out differently. He now seemed relieved as he eloquently expressed the deeply felt emotions that had been pent up for so long.

I too was relieved. What started as a fiasco with potentially dangerous prospects ended fortunately with astonishing insight, resolution of conflict, and a change in behavior. My office is now on the third floor, but the window is a regular sash type, fixed in position by an air conditioner. There is no balcony.

The Case That Taught
Me the Most

John F. McDermott, Jr., M.D.

I was a resident on the child psychiatry inpatient service, and my new patient was an 11-year-old abused youngster named Tom. He was admitted to the hospital because the community could no longer tolerate him. Expelled from school, he could not be managed in a foster home.

Of course, I expected Tom to welcome the chance to talk or play out his awful life experience with an understanding and knowledgeable adult! But he wouldn't talk about problems. And he certainly didn't view any of his *own* behavior as part of them. He had no vocabulary for putting feelings into words. When he experienced something, it was instantly translated into action—action that had a driven, urgent quality. Whenever I tried to focus on thoughts and feelings behind his behavior, the session disintegrated. There was no "observing part of the ego" I'd found so indispensable in work with adults.

Furthermore, Tom wouldn't even let me offer him a
"corrective emotional experience." We agreed on a handicap
in our checker games so that winning and losing would come
out about even. But after a few moves, the game was lost. It
would quickly extend beyond the checker board, and the
office became a battlefield. Swearing and cursing, he threw
checkers until the session ended—usually with him crawling
on the floor making animal noises. For him, a game of checkers was a matter of life or death. Checkers were "killed," not
jumped. Indeed, life was a matter of "kill or be killed." He
responded to the minimal rules in therapy as he responded to
those in checkers: He took pains to break them all! Nothing
seemed to work. The inevitable spiral of aggression was discouraging for a beginning therapist who began to dread the
coming of each therapy session.

But the driven, urgent quality of Tom's chaotic behavior
was a mystery to be solved. Patterns began to emerge—patterns that suggested an interior drama seeking a theater for
reenactment. His attacks alternated with challenges to attack
him. I began to draw attention to ways in which he tried to
bring about both hurting and being hurt.

A momentary breakthrough appeared after Tom cut his
hand and had to go to the hospital emergency room. An X
ray, two stitches, and a tetanus shot were enough to send
him away kicking and screaming at the top of his lungs.
Later, when I saw him, he was furious. X rays were dangerous! Emergency-room doctors were murderers! The bot-
tles of blood he saw were evidence they were bloodsuckers,
too! He worried that he might be given another shot at any
time. He wanted to know more in order to protect himself, so
we got a dummy syringe and began to play it out. Learning
how shots were given was a serious business, and it focused
his full concentration. Even the anatomy book was brought in
as a reference. When he was ready, we "cased" the emergen-

cy room together to see how it worked. (On the way back, he said the doctors there didn't look so huge and monstrous when you weren't being held down on the table looking up at them.)

Playing doctor was more than identification with the aggressor. It was also a way of enlisting Tom's cooperation in searching out the meaning of his behavior. The cycle of provocative behavior could be controlled and isolated when we played doctor. It was an avenue to explore the fears behind his chaotic behavior. When I recalled how he had challenged me to attack him, and how he must have been terrified at the same time, it triggered the unfolding memories of battles with his father. As we worked our way from behavior through the memories, he recalled his father's enraged brutality and his own confused terror. Like so many youngsters with borderline disorders, he feared the feeling of disintegration, or craziness, of being "not Tom." The "not Tom" feelings could now be understood. And with the relief in therapy, he could begin to pull himself together.

But of course the problem wasn't solved. Only the means had been discovered. Acting out hadn't stopped. True, it was under better control. But talking about doctors began to intensify his fear of me as well. After all, I was a doctor, too. And whenever he began to feel "forced"—to work in therapy—it was just like having a shot, and the session disintegrated. Once, at the end of an hour, he dropped to the floor behind my desk, swearing and cursing, daring me to carry him from the office. He was at a high pitch of excitement and wanted me to struggle with him. It was obvious that he had an erection, not just of his penis, but of his entire body. I left the room and he followed. But a therapeutic alliance had been forged, so in the next session we talked again about his fear of being attacked, which led to wild behavior. And now the excitement, too, could be explored. He didn't know why he did these things. But he was receptive to the notion that they could be a "way of talking" about things that were too frightening to remember, a way to get rid of scary memories by playing out the forgotten drama over and over again. Gradually, another story began to emerge—a story of sexual abuse. And the recollection was calming rather than frightening. Even school, which had been an extension of the battles with his father, began to shift into a learning and socialization experience. And for the first time, a game of checkers could be just a game of checkers!

Tom and I had both learned about transference in our therapeutic relationship. But we hadn't just discovered the phenomenon of acting out forgotten traumatic experiences; we had found ways to approach them so that current conflicts could be linked with conflicts locked up in the past and the mutually reinforcing pathology could be broken down into separate pieces that were no longer overwhelming. The real lesson had been in searching out what lay behind the acting out and discovering the underlying experiences of physical and sexual abuse.

It has become something of a cliché to say that we learn from our patients. But I learned the basic fundamentals of child psychotherapy from Tom, and from my supervisor, Selma Fraiberg.

How I Learned about Narcissism

Kenneth S. Robson, M.D.

Judith was a 10-year-old girl referred to me by her parents because of her teacher's increasing worry about her estrangement from other children in her public school classroom. She was an extremely intelligent but agitated child whose psychological thermostat seemed constantly set at the frenzy level. With one of my colleagues, I worked with Judith and her family for approximately 2 years. I saw her once weekly and met with her family approximately twice a month and, of course, worked closely with her school. While her therapy was helpful to her in many respects, the persistent experience that I as her therapist encountered was one of distance and difficulty in making good contact with her. This, of course, seemed to be the primary concern of her teacher, who initiated the referral. In such circumstances, with a child conveying such feelings, I experienced both boredom and drowsiness. Although I liked her and generally enjoyed my sessions with her, this aspect of them remained difficult.

After approximately 1 year of treatment, I was certain that there was a breakthrough! Judith indicated an interest in making picture puzzles with me, and I proceeded to purchase several that I was certain would captivate her fancy. At our first meeting after I purchased the puzzles, she proceeded to work diligently on one for most of the hour while I sat next to her. There was virtually no interaction between us, and she proceeded with her work quite content to have me by her side and physically quite out of reach. This scenario was then played out on a regular basis despite my invitations, imploring, clarifications and all the other tricks of our trade. Many months later in this same situation, she sat with her elbow virtually in my face. Suddenly, she turned to me and exclaimed, "You're not even helping me." I was searching for the right words to respond indignantly to this perception when she added, quietly, "I'm not letting you, am I?"

Judith's observation was a powerful one, and while it had little enduring influence in changing her basic orientation to the world, I found it highly instructive and valuable. It was humbling and demonstrated so clearly the dreadful durability of narcissistic defenses as they lead to an almost autistic posture vis-á-vis human relationships. Subsequently, Judith's self-observation seemed to recede into the deeper parts of her mind as her self-preoccupation and inaccessibility gradually modified. I suspect that I learned more from that brief glimmering of insight than she did.

"Happy Hanukkah"

John E. Schowalter, M.D.

I encountered this problem shortly after I finished training and had served the obligatory two years in the Army. One's first patients, referred by one's close colleagues and friends, are special. One is proving oneself worthy to be part of the professional community and to receive more referrals to fill up the blank spaces in one's appointment book.

This slight unease was present when I began to see 7-year-old David in September. He had minor fears of the dark, strangers, and new situations. These were bothersome, but not really incapacitating. He was also not doing as well in Jewish day school as his teachers and parents believed he should. He took too much time to be "perfect" and therefore did not get the work done. To his parents, he always seemed moderately unhappy and disgruntled. He was brought to treatment to see what seemed to be blocking him and whether anything could help him do better and feel better about himself. His father was an academician, his mother a housewife, and he had a brother 3 years younger than he who was reported to be doing well.

I saw David once a week. He was quite guarded. He spoke little and was not particularly interested in play. He occasionally brought books or other items from home or school. He made it clear that he had few friends and did not think of himself as very likeable. He believed other children resented his intelligence. His understanding of why he did only average in school was that he was bored and that it was probably obvious to all that he was one of the smartest boys in the class.

The incident to be discussed occurred a few months into the treatment. A month before Hanukkah, he began to talk about the gifts he expected to get. The emphasis was on whether or not these expectations would be fulfilled. I believed that a gift from me would also be appreciated and would probably strengthen a working alliance. I bought a small metal car similar to one that he did sometimes play with in the sessions and included with it a card saying "Happy Hanukkah." I gave it to him at the end of the session prior to the beginning of Hanukkah. His response was sudden and strong and occurred before he saw the gift—when he saw the card: I had misspelled Hanukkah, which should begin, he informed me, with the letter C. His anger was real. How could I be so uncaring, or ignorant, or anti-Semitic, or all of the above? My own reaction was of feeling flustered and defensive. Not knowing what to say, I said little (except that I did not think the C was that important) and looked uncomfortable.

As soon after the session as I could, I sought out a senior colleague who was familiar with Jewish custom and religion. I was brought up as a Lutheran in an area of the Midwest where there were no Jews. Since entering psychiatry, I had met many secular Jews, and I had recently moved into a largely Jewish neighborhood in which there were a substantial number of people who were moderately to profoundly religious. I was now aware enough of Jewish custom to know how complicated it was and how ignorant I was of many of the main points, much less the nuances. I felt I could not be sure that David was incorrect in his accusations. In our discussion, my wise colleague made a number of memorable points: First, a minority of Jewish therapists would spell Hanukkah with a *C*. Second, the first point did not necessarily mean that I was *not* uncaring, ignorant, anti-Semitic, or all of the above, but neither did my spelling necessarily indicate that I *was*. Countertransference must be delved into on one's own. Third, I was wrong to have said the *C* was unimportant. David's affect clearly belied that assumption. Fourth, I should read the paper on gift-giving by Temeles (1967). This paper succinctly discusses the pros, cons, and meanings of gift-giving between child and therapist.

In my next session with David, I was able to acknowledge that the spelling form was very meaningful to him and I was interested in how he felt. Over a number of sessions, it came out that he wondered whether I would naturally like him less than Gentile patients and whether I was so interested in Christmas that I had not paid sufficient attention to Hanukkah. A major theme of the rest of the therapy arose from the latter point. Christians care most for the Baby Jesus. David's parents cared more for his baby brother than for him. He was, in part, afraid to do as well as he could academically, because he believed young and needily acting children received better care.

So, the gift did strengthen the working alliance, but only after I learned better to accept affect immediately, while being more comfortable with the fact that it takes time to decipher its meanings.

A Case of Mental Retardation circa 1955

James E. Simmons, M.D.

Bobby, age 6½, was referred to us by his local school and his pediatrician for evaluation of learning and behavior problems.

A very careful diagnostic evaluation was done with weekly visits over a period of five or six weeks. This evaluation included a detailed and careful personal and developmental history, a family history of the parents and the extended family, a review of the child's school records and a conference with his teacher, a 2-hour psychiatric examination of the child, and formal psychological testing. A diagnosis of uncomplicated mild mental retardation (I.Q. approximately 60) was made. Bobby himself was a rather engaging child who was somewhat distressed that he had trouble learning the academic subjects, that he was frequently teased by the other children, and, most recently, that he had been excluded from school. The main problem for this author was dealing with the parents and helping them understand Bobby's plight.

It is important to put this case in historical perspective. At the time I saw Bobby, most retarded children were sheltered by their families and hidden from public view. Professionals and lay persons alike had a very dim outlook on the prognosis for these children ever reaching an independent, productive life in adulthood. The Kennedy family had not yet openly acknowledged their retarded child, and the public schools in most parts of the country offered very little or no help to these children or their families. Special classes for the retarded were considered not very useful and an expensive luxury that the district schools simply could not afford. The public schools for the most part did not consider the handicapped child their responsibility. These children were time-consuming for the teachers and often disruptive in the classroom. Most school administrators wanted them out of the school and had few, if any, alternative suggestions. Actually, there were a few training centers in the private sector, some quite expensive but others sponsored by philanthropic groups and within the reach of many families, though not all. The state training schools for the mentally retarded were, of course, available to all citizens. However, they were inadequately staffed and overcrowded and had a very bad reputation that made most families loath to place their children in them except as a very last resort.

Bobby's parents had adamantly denied that he had any problems throughout the diagnostic evaluation and made it quite clear they expected a letter to be written to the school board saying the child was mentally normal and must be reinstated in the school. Of all the examinations given to Bobby, he had scored at age level or a little above on the

Goodenough Draw-A-Person procedure. However, when he drew the person, he drew it upside down. That is, he started with the head at the bottom of his sheet of paper and drew upward so that the legs were at the top of the page. We asked him who had taught him to draw such a nice picture of a person. He said that his mother had shown him how to do it. The mother denied that she had taught him to draw. However, we suspected that she had not only taught him but also coached him intensively. Unfortunately, she did not sit beside him as she taught him to draw. She sat across the table from him, so that when he followed her maneuvers, he drew the figure upside down, just as he saw his mother draw a figure. He did not seem to be aware that his figure was upside down, but it did have all the necessary components.

One of the reasons for seeing a child and the family several times at weekly intervals is to help the parents, through a review of their child's symptoms and development, come to a better understanding of the basis of the child's problem and be ready to hear a diagnosis and to make some realistic plans about helping the child. We always hope to lead the parents to some kind of diagnostic understanding, no matter what the final diagnosis may be.

When I met with Bobby's parents in the disposition conference, I asked them my usual questions concerning how Bobby had been doing over the last few weeks and what kind of things they had come to see as possible reasons for his problems. I met with stony silence. His mother said that he had no problems and that he was being misjudged by an incompetent school staff. The father volunteered no opinions at all. When he was asked, he stated that he thought that he probably agreed with his wife, for she was with Bobby more and he believed she understood and knew their son better. He simply did not understand why the school said Bobby couldn't learn and why they excluded him from attendance.

The parents had honestly given us Bobby's developmental history, which was seriously delayed in almost every area. It is true that he was their only child, but it was hard to believe they had never looked at a child-rearing book or at friends' or relatives' children and seen how far behind his age group he really was.

In my own feelings, I was quite torn. I could not honestly say that Bobby had average abilities and should be in regular school classes. However, I personally felt it was very wrong that schools should be permitted to turn their backs on these handicapped children. Many of my colleagues at the time felt that these children most certainly were educable and should not be excluded from the mainstream or "warehoused" in institutions. We felt that if these children were accurately diagnosed to the parents and to the public, school systems could no longer say that the numbers of such children were insignificant and refuse them education services. I was realistic enough to know that such a social change could not be brought about by the relatively few child mental health professionals in communities. Such changes would have to be brought about by the parents and the citizens with support from the professionals. I knew that if I lied in my report, saying Bobby had normal intelligence, I still could not force the school to take him back, and I felt such action would be cruel to him, exposing him to more frustration in a situation with which he could not cope.

Therefore, I set about trying to educate Bobby's parents. I spent considerable time reviewing his delayed development, even though we did not know the causes of this delay. I reviewed the psychological test findings. I talked about chronological age and mental age, and I used such euphemisms as "slow learner" and "limitations in his ability to master academic matters." Looking back on the conference later, I believe I had been afraid to use the word "retardation" to his mother.

Then I remembered having recently read *The Child Who Never Grew* by Pearl Buck, the story of her own pain and anguish as she went from doctor to doctor and from city to city to find out why her child was not growing socially and mentally. With considerable insight, Ms. Buck reviewed her own massive denial of the facts before her face and of her inability to hear the doctor's diagnoses or their recommendations. She then told of one doctor in a large medical center in the Midwest who examined her child and then took her aside and told her that she was blind to the real issues and was not hearing anyone's diagnosis because she wanted her child to be declared normal. He made her look him in the eye, and he told her that her child was not normal and was suffering from mental retardation. Ms. Buck became overwhelmed with her own emotions. She cried. She accused the doctor of being cruel, of being incompetent, but he held his ground. She said later she came to realize that this man was the kindest of all. He helped her finally come to accept her child's problems and to do something constructive about it.

As I say, in reflecting on how I might help Bobby's mother I remembered what I had read in this book. Possibly out of my own frustration, but I hope with the kindest of intentions, I told Bobby's mother that I would not write a letter to the school, that Bobby was not normal, and that he did suffer mental retardation. At this point, the mother uttered a short cry, stood up, and began walking rapidly around my room in circles, not looking at anyone, but saying, "Lies, lies, lies, lies." I got her attention and asked her if she thought I was lying and if she thought I would lie about something as serious as this—whereupon she turned on her heel, walked out of my office, and ran down the hall. During this interchange, the child's father sat there without saying a word or even moving in his chair. I looked at him in, I guess, a questioning way, and he responded, "She tends to get overwrought sometimes." He still had not moved. I agreed with him and asked that he go to her. He left the room, and after a few minutes both he and his wife left our clinic.

At this writing, I simply cannot remember what happened to Bobby and his family. It was a very strong emotional experience for me. I felt a deep sense of failure, not that I was unable to make an accurate diagnosis, but that I was unable to convey our findings to the family and offer some sort of help.

Freud once said that for an interpretation to have therapeutic effect, it must meet two requirements: (1) It must be correct and (2) it must be stated at a time when the patient is capable of hearing and understanding it. The same could be said for treatment planning. We must not only have the correct diagnosis, but also convey the diagnosis and remedial requirements to the patient and family when they are ready to accept it.

I can't be sure exactly what I would do differently if Bobby's mother came to me today, but I would be different. Most certainly I would give her much more of my time, at least a few more visits, to try to form a more workable relationship with her. I also know that my knowledge and probably my attitudes about mental retardation have changed a great deal. More important, I am grateful that today the community at large, both professional and nonprofessional, has recognized and learned that "simple, uncomplicated mental retardation" is seldom, if ever, simple or uncomplicated. We can now understand the retarded child better and truly identify with his or her parents. Professionals, including myself, now have broader knowledge, so that we can help the parents with a prognosis based on objective facts rather than our own positive or negative feelings about prognosis. Much more important than any change in myself or any other professional is the fact that public policy now acknowledges the presence of retarded children. Only a short time ago, federal and state laws were passed mandating that local schools provide educational services for the emotionally and mentally handicapped child. The Bobbys of this country can no longer legally be sent home by the school principal. Having the law and enforcing it are not the same, but having the law is progress in the right direction.

Henry

Edward Sperling, M.D.

At our first meeting, Henry, age 5½, left his mother in the waiting room and, without glancing back at her, came with me into my office. He was a slim boy of medium height, whose dark curly hair framed a thin, pale face. His dark eyes were set close together, giving his expression a sharp, piercing quality. His glances, however, were infrequent as he kept his head bowed even after he was seated at the play table. He was obviously ill at ease, not looking at me and mumbling softly to himself. I showed him some of my play material—doll furniture, construction toys, puppets, a ball—to no avail. He hardly looked at them, just as he avoided looking at me, but continued to gaze at the table and intermittently speak to himself.

The few words I caught gave me the impression that Henry's thoughts were disorganized and that he was preoccupied with lights. When I commented that he seemed interested in lights, he flinched, seemed frightened, and mentioned something about lights being broken. I told him that broken lights could be frightening, but perhaps they didn't have to remain frightening—but attempts to pursue this track were in vain.

With some feeling of desperation, I asked Henry whether he would like to draw something, and he nodded assent. He then carefully drew a road map, indicating the network of highways that surround the area of my office. I asked which highway he took to come to me, and he carefully drew the route from his home to my office, correctly naming all the side roads, highways, and interchanges on the way. Although he was more animated while doing the drawing, his speech was terse, without emotional inflection, high-pitched, and tense. His facial expression was inwardly directed and grim. When I commented on his unusual knowledge of roads and directions, he seemed to relax a little in his body posture, but continued to look at the play table. I then showed him an automobile highway map. He quickly spread it out on the play table and pointed out on it the roads he had previously drawn. By now, the session was drawing to a close, and with some remarks about how we would meet regularly and get to know each other better, I delivered him back to his mother, feeling that we had set out on an unmarked road to making contact. This tentative, fragile contact was soon to change character and to present other problems in our being together.

Henry was the first child of a middle-class professional family. He was an eagerly wanted child, his mother having readily interrupted her career to stay home and raise him. The first 2 years of his life went smoothly, but at age 2½, when his beloved neighbors moved away, he became very distraught, and frightened, and his well-developing speech deteriorated into broken fragments. After a few weeks, he seemed to recover and several months later began nursery school. In school, he was isolated, preferring to play re-petitively by himself, and preoccupied with a record about a song having to do with someone moving away. After a few months, he made some slight progress in socializing, but throughout the second year, his progress was slow, so that a special school was recommended. At age 5, he was enrolled in a fine private school, but after a few weeks, the school refused to keep him because his social behavior was too aberrant. This rejection precipitated his psychiatric treatment.

During the early part of the treatment, Henry exhibited his preoccupations with broken things, especially lights but also including statues, machines, and other inanimate objects. He was intensely preoccupied with bowel movements and the possibility of soiling himself. While drawing scenes of broken lights, bowel movements, and other concerns, he would become excited, jumping up and down, shrieking with excitement, pleasure, and anxiety—all blended together. He was able to tell me about an episode of soiling at age 2 (verified by his mother), and we were able to link his preoccupation with broken objects to worries about his body exploding (when he was constipated) or falling apart. As he became more related, he developed a pattern of not wanting the sessions to end. Even though I alerted him in advance that we had "five minutes to finish up" and reassured him that treatment was regular and ongoing, he would show his displeasure and anxiety in impulsive, primitive ways. He would attempt to scribble on the wall or would throw toys on the floor. Once he tried to urinate on the floor and, when I intervened, wrapped himself in a drape to prevent me from stopping him. Very often, the sessions ended with my having to envelop him until he was calm enough to leave. After an initial struggle, he would ultimately relax and allow me to conduct him out of the office in a relatively calm state. I sometimes had the impression that he enjoyed being held, because he seemed to provoke this kind of interaction, despite the struggles that followed.

During his various "separation struggles," Henry never broke any of my office furnishings, until one day he seized the glass insert of a large round wooden ashtray and smashed it to the floor. This action was accompanied by his usual excited laughter and jumping up and down. I decided to replace the glass insert and to keep a sharp eye on him toward the end of each session, but this plan was thrown into disarray when Henry, upon first spying it, smashed the second insert.

I was caught in a dilemma. I felt that if I replaced the ashtray with an unbreakable one, I might be giving Henry the message that he could never master his impulses and that the world would have to accommodate itself to him. On the other hand, it made no sense to challenge him and myself with another breakable insert. I felt I had to find a balance between respecting the intact part of his ego and protecting him from the destruction resulting from his aggressive impulses. After buying a new glass insert, I told him that I had replaced the insert but that I would place the ashtray on a shelf, beyond his reach, until I felt he was under sufficient control not to break it. He accepted this arrangement without a word, and we continued to work on separation issues (and many other issues) by making a calendar together, marking the dates of our sessions months in advance, and keeping the calendar up to date as the weeks went by. After an initial attempt to reach the glass insert, now out of his reach, he lost interest in it and did not try to break any other furnishings in the office.

As several months passed, Henry's separation struggles gradually diminished, and I wondered when and how I would know he was ready to deal with the ashtray. One day some 5 months after he had broken the last insert, in the middle of one of our sessions, I noticed that I had forgotten to place the ashtray up on the customary shelf. He didn't seem to notice, and I left well enough alone. From then on, the ashtray remained within easy reach, and it was never an issue again. As happens so often in therapy, a not-so-conscious perception or intuition shaped the intervention.

Epilogue

The treatment of such a severely ego-deviant child required a long-term, comprehensive environmental and pharmacological approach in which psychotherapy was only one element. Henry was in therapy, with gradually diminishing intensity, for some ten years. Toward the latter half of high school, he was able to stop regular sessions and see me on and off as difficulties arose. He attended a special therapeutic school until junior high school, then switched to public school, where with the help of guidance personnel he was eventually able to graduate from high school. He then successfully obtained a college degree, though there continued to be instances, similar to the ashtray episode, when the fragile balance between his disturbed social perceptions, his impulses, and his observing ego put him in jeopardy.

4

Concluding Comments

We and our contributors have described a variety of difficult moments in psychotherapy with children. We have defined a difficult moment as a concrete expression of a disparity between the therapist's and the child's or the parents' expectations of the treatment process. A difficult moment captures the manifest and symbolic meaning of these conflicted expectations. Difficult moments will invariably occur at some time in the therapy with a child.

Difficult moments can have varied impacts on the process of child psychotherapy. For example, the difficult moment when a child refuses to enter the treatment room may determine whether treatment can occur at all. On a more symbolic level, a child who brings food to a session may be indicating that he or she is satisfied and comfortable with treatment and that the process should continue. It is essential that the therapist understand the child's manifest behavior and its symbolic meaning in managing a difficult moment in child psychotherapy. Some difficult moments may occur only once, but others may occur repeatedly in the work with a given child. Assessment of this trend can help the therapist unlock the mysteries of the child's conflicts that necessitated treatment.

It must be clearly recognized by all therapists who work with children that difficult moments are inevitable. Experience does help in developing skill in managing them. In addition, a therapist ought to be open and agreeable about seeking advice from a colleague or supervisor about problems in managing children's difficult moments in psychotherapy. At times, therapists may wish to explore, in their own psycho-therapy, issues about potential countertransference reactions that involve unconscious reactions that arise in their work with children (Bornstein, 1984; Winnicott, 1949; Tower, 1956; Berlin, 1973, 1986; Kabcenell, 1974; Marshall, 1979; Furman, 1980; Pfeffer and Plutchik, 1982; Spurlock, 1985).

Finally, difficult moments are sometimes frustrating but always challenging events! They stimulate the therapist to think rapidly and to integrate previously accrued knowledge about the child with newly perceived facets of the difficult moment. They may be pivotal times in the therapy for the child and for the parents. They test our skill as therapists and often provide a means to further our helpful work with children.

References

Adams, P. (1974): *A Primer of Child Psychotherapy*. Boston: Little, Brown.

Alger, I., Linn, S., and Beardslee, W. (1985): Puppetry as a therapeutic tool for hospitalized children. *Hospital and Community Psychiatry* 36(2):129–130.

Anthony, E. J. (1964): Communicating therapeutically with the child. *Journal of the American Academy of Child Psychiatry* 3:109–110.

Barrett, C. L., Hampe, I. E., and Miller, L. C. (1978): Research on child psychotherapy. In *Handbook of Psychotherapy and Behavior Change*, 2nd ed. S. L. Garfield and A. E. Bergin, eds. New York: John Wiley, pp. 411–435.

Beitchman, J., and Dielman, T. (1983): Terminators and remainers in child psychiatry: The patient–treatment fit. *Journal of Clinical Psychiatry* 44:413–416.

Bender, L., and Woltmann, A. G. (1952): Puppet shows as a psychotherapeutic method. In *Child Psychiatric Techniques*. L. Bender, ed. Springfield, Illinois: Charles C Thomas, pp. 238–257.

Berlin, I. N. (1973): Parental blame: An obstacle in psychotherapeutic work with schizophrenic children and their families. In *Clinical Studies in Childhood Psychoses*. S. A. Szurek and I.N. Berlin, eds. New York: Brunner/Mazel, pp. 115–126.

Berlin, I. N. (1986): Clinical experience: Some transference and countertransference issues in the playroom. *Journal of the American Academy of Child & Adolescent Psychiatry* 26(1):101–107.

Bernal, M. E., Klinnert, M. D., and Schultz, L. A. (1980): Outcome evaluation of behavioral parent training and client-centered parent counseling for children with conduct problems. *Journal of Applied Behavior Analysis* 13:677–691.

Bornstein, B. (1984): Emotional barriers in the understanding and treatment of young children. *American Journal of Orthopsychiatry* 18:691–697.

Brody, S. (1961): Transference resistance in pre-puberty. *The Psychoanalytic Study of the Child* 16:251–274.

Cantor, S., and Kestenbaum, C. (1986): Psychotherapy with schizophrenic children. *Journal of the American Academy of Child Psychiatry* 25(5):623–630.

Carek, D. J. (1972): *Principles of Child Psychotherapy.* Springfield, Illinois: Charles C Thomas.

Casey, R. J., and Berman, J. S. (1985): The outcome of psychotherapy with children. *Psychological Bulletin* 98(2):388–400.

Claman, L. (1980): The squiggle-drawing game in child psychotherapy. *American Journal of Psychotherapy* 34(3):414–425.

D'Angelo, R. Y., and Walsh, J. F. (1967): An evaluation of various therapy approaches with lower socioeconomic-group children. *Journal of Psychology* 67:59–64.

Dulcan, M. K. (1984): Brief psychotherapy with children and their families: The state of the art. *Journal of the American Academy of Child Psychiatry* 23(5):544–551.

Fraiberg, S. (1962): Transference aspects of the analysis of a child with a severe behavior disorder. *Journal of the American Psychoanalytical Association* 10:338–367.

Frank, J. (1976): Restoration of morale and behavior change. In *What Makes Behavior Change Possible?* A. Burton, ed. New York: Brunner/Mazel, pp. 73–95.

Freud, A. (1964): The ego and the mechanisms of defense. In *The Writings of Anna Freud*, Vol. 2. New York: International Universities Press, pp. 25–26.

Freud, A. (1965): *Normality and Pathology in Childhood.* New York: International Universities Press.

Freud, A. (1966): *Normality and Pathology in Childhood: Assessments of Development.* London: Hogarth Press.

Freud, S. (1962): The dynamics of transference. In *Standard Edition*, Vol. 12. London: Hogarth Press, pp. 97–108.

Furman, E. (1980): Transference and externalization in latency. *The Psychoanalytic Study of the Child* 35:267–284.

Gardner, R. (1971): *Therapeutic Communication with Children: The Mutual Story-Telling Technique.* New York: Jason Aronson.

Gardner, R. (1972): Mutual story telling technique in the treatment of anger: Inhibition problems. *International Journal of Child Psychotherapy* 1(1):34–64.

Gardner, R. (1975): *Psychotherapeutic Approaches to the Resistant Child.* New York: Jason Aronson.

Gluck, M. R., Tanner, M. M., Sullivan, D. F., and Erickson, P. A. (1964): Follow-up evaluation of 55 child guidance cases. *Behavior Research and Therapy*, 2:131–134.

Griest, D. L., Forehand, R., Rogers, T., Breiner, J., Furey, W., and Williams, C. A. (1982): Effects of parent enhancement therapy on the treatment outcome and generalization of parent training program. *Behavior Research and Therapy* 20:429–436.

Group for the Advancement of Psychiatry—Committee on Child Psychiatry (1982): *The Process of Child Therapy.* New York: Brunner/Mazel.

Haworth, M., ed. (1964): *Child Psychotherapy: Practice and Theory.* New York: Basic Books.

Haworth, M. R. (1968): Doll play and puppetry. In *Projective Techniques in Personality Assessment.* A. I. Rabin, ed. New York: Springer, pp. 327–365.

Heinicke, C. M. (1965): Frequency of psychotherapeutic session as a factor affecting the child's developmental status. *The Psychopathology of the Child* 20:42–98.

Heinicke, C. M. (1969): Frequency of psychotherapeutic session as a factor affecting outcome. *Journal of Abnormal Psychology* 74:553–560.

Heinicke, C. M. and Ramsey-Klee, D. M. (1968): Outcome of child psychotherapy as a function of frequency of session. *Journal of the American Academy of Child Psychiatry* 25(2):247–253.

Heinicke, C. M., and Strassman, L. H. (1975): Toward more effective research on child psychotherapy. *Journal of the American Academy of Child Psychiatry* 14:561–588.

Hicks, D. F. (1974): Supershrink: Methods of a therapist judged successful on the basis of adult outcomes of adolescent patients. In *Life History Research in Psychopathology*, Vol. 3. D. F. Ricks, A.

Thomas, and M. Roff, eds. Minneapolis: University of Minnesota Press, pp. 275–297.

Horenstein, D., and Hauston, B. (1976): The expectation–reality discrepancy and premature termination from psychotherapy. *Journal of Clinical Therapy* 60:326–329.

Howlin, P. A., Marchant, R., Rutter, M., Berger, M., Hersov, L., and Yule, W. (1973): A home-based approach to the treatment of autistic children. *Journal of Autism and Childhood Schizophrenia* 3:308–336.

Howlin, P. A., Marchant, R., Rutter, M., Berger, M., Hersov, L., and Yule, W. (1984): Treatment of conduct disorders. In *Psychotherapy Research: Where Are We and Where Should We Go?* New York: Guilford, pp. 3–28.

Kabcenell, R. (1974): On countertransference. *The Psychoanalytic Study of the Child* 29:22–33.

Kazdin, A. E., and Wilson, G. T. (1978): Criteria for evaluating psychotherapy. *Archives of General Psychiatry* 35:407–416.

Klein, M. (1973): *The Psychoanalysis of Children.* London: Hogarth Press.

Kolvin, I., Garside, R. F., Nicol, A. R., MacMillan, A., Wolstenholme, F., and Leitch, I.M. (1981): *Help Starts Here: The Maladjusted Child in the Ordinary School.* London: Tavistock.

Lamp, S. (1986): Treating sexually abused children: Issues of blame and responsibility. *American Journal of Orthopsychiatry* 56(2):303–307.

Levinson, R. B., and Kitchener, H. L. (1966): Treatment of delinquents. *Journal of Consulting Clinical Psychology* 30:364.

Levitt, E. E. (1957): The results of psychotherapy with children. *Behavior Research and Therapy* 60:326–329.

Levitt, E. E. (1963): Psychotherapy with children: A further evaluation. *Behavior Research and Therapy* 60:326–329.

Looney, J. G. (1984): Treatment planning in child psychiatry. *Journal of the American Academy of Child Psychiatry* 23(5):529–536.

Markowitz, J. (1964): The nature of child's initial resistance to psychotherapy. In *Child Psychotherapy.* M. R. Harworth, ed. New York: Basic Books, pp. 186–193.

Marshall, R. J. (1979): Countertransference in the psychotherapy of children and adolescents. In *Countertransference: The Therapist's Contribution to Treatment.* L. Epstein and A. J. Feiner, eds. New York: Jason Aronson, pp. 595–628.

McAdoo, W. and Roeske, N. (1973): A comparison of defectors and continuers in a child guidance clinic. *Journal of Consulting Clinical Psychology* 40:328–334.

McConville, B. J. (1976): Opening moves and sequential strategies in child psychotherapy. *Canadian Psychiatry Association Journal* 21:295–301.

McDermott, J. F., and Char, W. F. (1984): Stage-related models of psychotherapy with children. *Journal of the American Academy of Child Psychiatry* 23(5):537–543.

McDermott, J., and Harrison, S., eds. (1977): *Psychiatric Treatment of the Child*. New York: Jason Aronson.

Norick, T., Benson, R., and Rembar, T. (1981): Patterns of termination in an outpatient clinic for children and adolescents. *Journal of the American Academy of Child Psychiatry* 20:834–844.

Olden, C. (1953): On adult empathy with children. *The Psychoanalytic Study of the Child* 8:111–126.

Ornstein, A. (1976): Making contact with the inner world of the child: Toward a theory of psychoanalytic psychotherapy with children. *Comprehensive Psychiatry* 17:3–36.

Ornstein, A. (1981): Self pathology in childhood: Developmental and clinical considerations. *Psychiatric Clinics of North America* 4:435–453.

Oster, G. D., and Gould, P. (1987): *Using Drawings in Assessment and Therapy*. New York: Brunner/Mazel.

Patterson, G. R. (1974): Interventions of boys with conduct problems: Multiple settings, treatments and criteria. *Journal of Consulting Clinical Psychology* 42:471–481.

Pfeffer, C. R. (1984): Modalities of treatment for suicidal children: An overview of the literature on current practice. *American Journal of Psychotherapy* 38(3):364–372.

Pfeffer, C. R. (1986): *The Suicidal Child*. New York: Guilford.

Pfeffer, C. R., and Plutchik, R. (1982): Psychopathology of latency-age children: Relation to treatment planning. *Journal of Nervous and Mental Disease* 17:193–197.

Powell, G. J. (1973): Self-concept in white and black children. In *Racism and Mental Health*. C. V. Willie, B. M. Kraine, and S. Brown, eds. Pittsburgh: University of Pittsburgh Press, pp. 299–318.

Pruett, K. D., and Dahl, E. K. (1982): Psychotherapy of gender identity conflict in young boys. *Journal of the American Academy of Child Psychiatry* 21(1):65–70.

Reisinger, J. J., Frangia, G. W., and Hoffman, E. H. (1976): Toddler management training: Generalization and marital status. *Journal of Behavior Therapy and Experimental Psychology* 7:335–340.

Ross, A. D., and Lacey, H. M. (1961): Characteristics of terminators and remainers in child guidance treatment. *Journal of Consulting Psychology* 25:420–424.

Rutter, M. (1981a): *Maternal Deprivation Reassessed*, 2nd ed. Harmondsworth, England: Penguin.

Rutter, M. (1981b): Stress, coping and development: Some issues and some questions. *Journal of Child Psychology and Psychiatry* 22:323–356.

Schaffer, D. (1984): Notes on psychotherapy research among children and adolescents. *Journal of the American Academy of Child Psychiatry* 23(5):552–561.

Shapiro, I. E. (1975): Puppetry as a diagnostic and therapeutic technique. *Psychiatry and Art* 4:86–94.

Shapiro, T., and Esman, A. H. (1985): Psychotherapy with children and adolescents: Still relevant in the 1980s? *Psychiatric Clinics of North America* 8(4):909–921.

Small, A. C., and Teagno, L. J. (1980): The child's and parents' expectations of psychotherapy. *Developmental and Behavioral Pediatrics* 1(2):74–77.

Spurlock, J. (1985): Assessment and therapeutic intervention of black children. *Journal of the American Academy of Child Psychiatry* 24(2):168–174.

Stirtzinger, R. M. (1983): Story telling: A creative therapeutic technique. *Canadian Journal of Psychiatry* 28:561–565.

Strain, M. L., Glass, G. V., and Miller, T. L. (1980): *The Benefits of Psychotherapy*. Baltimore: Johns Hopkins University Press.

Strupp, H. H. (1975): Psychoanalysis, "focal psychotherapy" and the nature of the therapeutic influence. *Archives of General Psychiatry* 132:127–135.

Swanson, L., and Biaggio, M. K. (1985): Therapeutic perspectives on father–daughter incest. *American Journal of Psychiatry* 142:667–674.

Taylor, R. L. (1976): Psychosocial development among children and youth: A reexamination. *American Journal of Orthopsychiatry* 46:4–19.

Temeles, M. S. (1967): Gift giving. *Bulletin of the Philadelphia Association of Psycho-Analysis* 17:31–32.

Tseng, W. S., and McDermott, J. F. (1975): Psychotherapy: Historical roots, universal elements and cultural variations. *American Journal of Psychiatry* 132:378–384.

Tower, L. E. (1956): Countertransference. *Journal of the American Psychoanalytic Association* 6:224–255.

Traux, C. B., and Carlshuff, R. R. (1967): *Towards Effective Counseling and Psychotherapy: Training and Practice*. Chicago: Aldine.

Weisz, J. R. (1986): Contingency and control beliefs as predictors of psychotherapy outcomes among children and adolescents. *Journal of Consulting and Clinical Psychology* 54(6):789–795.

Whitten, C. F., Pettit, M. G., and Fischoff, J. (1969): Evidence that failure from maternal deprivation is secondary to undereating. *Journal of the American Medical Association* 209:1675–1682.

Winnicott, D. W. (1949): Hate in the countertransference. *International Journal of Psychoanalysis* 30:69–77.

Winnicott, D. W. (1971): *Therapeutic Communication in Child Psychiatry*. London: Hogarth.

Wright, D. M., Moelis, I., and Pollack, L. J. (1976): The outcome of individual child psychotherapy: Increments at follow-up. *Journal of Child Psychology and Psychiatry* 17:275–285.

Yarrow, L. J., and Harmon, R. J. (1980): Maternal deprivation. In *Comprehensive Textbook of Psychiatry*, Vol. III. Baltimore: Wilkins and Wilkins, pp. 2727–2734.

Index